2048

Humanity's Agreement to Live Together

J. Kirk Boyd

16
EasyRead Large

RHYW

Copyright Page from the Original Book

2048

Berrett-Koehler Publishers, Inc.
235 Montgomery Street, Suite 650
San Francisco, California 94104-2916
Tel: (415) 288-0260, Fax: (415) 362-2512
www.bkconnection.com

Ordering information for print editions
Quantity sales. Special discounts are available on quantity purchases by corporations, associations, and others. For details, contact the "Special Sales Department" at the Berrett-Koehler address above.
Individual sales. Berrett-Koehler publications are available through most bookstores. They can also be ordered directly from Berrett-Koehler: Tel: (800) 929-2929; Fax: (802) 864-7626; www.bkconnection.com
Orders for college textbook/course adoption use. Please contact Berrett-Koehler: Tel: (800) 929-2929; Fax: (802) 864-7626.
Orders by U.S. trade bookstores and wholesalers. Please contact Ingram Publisher Services, Tel: (800) 509-4887; Fax: (800) 838-1149; E-mail: customer.service@ingrampublisherservices.com; or visit www.ingram publisherservices.com/Ordering for details about electronic ordering.

First Edition
Hardcover print edition ISBN 978-1-60509-539-4
Paperback print edition ISBN 978-1-60509-330-7
PDF e-book ISBN 978-1-60509-331-4
IDPF e-book ISBN 978-1-60509-803-6

2010-1

Project management by Michael Bass Associates.
2048 logo design by Carla Radostra.
Cover design by Pemastudio.
Book design and composition by Valerie Brewster, Scribe Typography.

This optimized ReadHowYouWant edition contains the complete, unabridged text of the original publisher's edition. Other aspects of the book may vary from the original edition.

Set in 16 pt. Verdana

TABLE OF CONTENTS

More Praise for 2048

"All great human achievement seems impossible until it happens, and then it was inevitable. *2048* offers us the gift of advanced hindsight. The book provides one vision for how future generations may look back and see just how we met the great challenge of securing human rights in all nations."

—The Honorable Jeffrey L. Bleich, former Special Counsel to the President of the United States

"Kirk Boyd's vision of a global, binding human rights compact underpinned by a system of courts of law, or an International Court of Human Rights, is not just one of the many possible future scenarios. It is essential if international law is to make the quantum leap from a mere system of laws to a true legal order."

—Cesare Romano, Professor, Loyola Law School, and Assistant Director, Project on International Courts and Tribunals

"There is nothing more fundamental than for humanity to reach an agreement to live together. The European Convention on Human Rights already works for forty-seven countries. Kirk Boyd points the way to a universal approach along similar lines."

—Jurriaan Kamp, publisher, *Ode*

"It's time for economic and social rights such as education and health care for women and men in all countries—*2048* shows how we might achieve this goal."

—Joan Blades, cofounder, MoveOn.org and MomsRising.org

"*2048* has a grand participatory vision, which will change not only the way we view the world but the way we interact with it and with each other. It is a project that must succeed if we are to have a more decent human future."

—David Krieger, President, Nuclear Age Peace Foundation

"People working for social change should read *2048.* It gives a new perspective on how some of the resources currently channeled toward solving the problems arising from our flawed existing social order might be better repurposed toward restructuring the system that is creating these problems. *2048* shows the way."

—Caroline Avery, President, Durfee Foundation

"Human rights are a permanent vocation. Even after the wonderful work of codification by the United Nations and of the regional human rights commissions and courts, reflection goes on because we need better mechanisms of implementation, such as the World Court of Human Rights envisaged by Project 2048. This is a noble task that should reflect the views of all of humanity, including the approaches of the thinkers and lawyers of Central and South America."

—Jose Ayala Lasso, first United Nations High Commissioner for Human Rights

"It's heartening to see a global dialogue developing through *2048* that can lead humanity to an agreement to live together. With this inspiring, visionary book, Kirk Boyd not only raises awareness of the unfolding 2048 story, he provides a catalyst for people all over the world to join in the conversation themselves."

—John Esterle, Executive Director, Whitman Institute

"Many great, but unenforceable, legal opinions have been written by the committees within the United Nations. It's time for a project such as 2048 that will build enforceable decisions upon this foundation."

—Alfred de Zayas, legal counsel for the United Nations Human Rights Committee

"Harry Truman wanted there to be an International Bill of Rights, and I'm glad to see one coming into existence through the 2048 Project."

—Frank Kelly, author and speechwriter for President Truman

"I'm glad to be working through 2048 to equip barristers in all countries with an International Bill of Rights they can use to enforce rights in their courts of law."

—James J. Brosnahan, Trial Lawyer, Morrison & Foerster

"Boyd proposes an ambitious new social contract for humanity that could serve as a tipping point for enforcing human rights worldwide."

—Jill Van den Brule, Communications Specialist, Education and Gender Equality, UNICEF, and international child rights advocate

This book is dedicated to my parents—John Boyd, an architect who never saw walls, just possibilities, and taught me to do the same with law, and Betsy Roberts and David Roberts, a teacher and professor who taught me to look at humanity as well as myself.

***

To the people of the State of California, who, by creating and paying for the University of California system, have given me the opportunity for a rich, fulfilling life. I'm working to give back.

***

And to the judges sitting in courts at all levels and in all countries who represent much of the best of human character: impartiality, justice, and dedication to the rule of law. Our agreement to live together belongs in your hands to enforce.

TIMELINE FOR THE ACHIEVEMENT OF THE 2048 PROJECT

1933 Nazis begin using concentration camps. Holocaust underway.

1941 President Roosevelt outlines Four Freedoms in State of the Union address.

1945 U.N. Charter signed.

1946 U.N. Commission on Human Rights created.

1948 Universal Declaration of Human Rights adopted by U.N. General Assembly.

1950 European Convention on Human Rights adopted by Council of Europe.

1953 International Law Commission begins drafting Statute for International Criminal Court.

1966 Covenant on Economic, Social, and Cultural Rights and Covenant on Civil and Political Rights adopted by United Nations.

1969 American Convention on Human Rights adopted by Organization of American States.

1976 Covenant on Economic, Social, and Cultural Rightsand Covenant on Civil and Political Rights enter into force.

1978 American Convention on Human Rights enters into force.

1979 Inter-American Court of Human Rights established.

1981 African Charter on Human and Peoples' Rights adopted by Organization of African Unity.

1986 African Charter on Human and Peoples' Rights enters into force.

1996 Statute of International Criminal Court adopted following Rwandan Genocide.

2004 African Court on Human and Peoples' Rights created.

2008 2048 Project launched. Swiss government launches Agenda for Human Rights. Arab Charter on Human Rights enters into force.

2010 Swiss Agenda for Human Rights presents statute for World Court of Human Rights.

2011 U.N. Human Rights Council should create working group to draft International Convention on Human Rights.

2012 International Law Commission (ILC) begins draft of International Convention on Human Rights.2048 Conference for Review of Draft International Convention on Human Rights.

2013 Human Rights Council Working Group presents draft International Convention on Human Rights.

2014 International Law Commission presents draft International Convention on Human Rights.

2015 2048 Second Conference on Draft International Convention on Human Rights.

2017 Rome Conference to combine U.N. Working Group draft, ILC draft, 2048 draft, and Swiss Agenda statute.

2018 World Trade Organization should pass a resolution requiring all state parties to ratify the International Convention on Human Rights in order to maintain their membership status.

2020 International Convention on Human Rights enters into force.

2022 Regional Courts expanded and established to hear cases based on International Convention on Human Rights.

2025 Cases begin to percolate through the regional courts up to the International Court of Human Rights.

2030 Domestic, regional, and international courts enforce International Convention on Human Rights.

2048 Well established body of domestic, regional and international case law ensuring the enforcement of the International Convention on Human Rights in the courts of all countries.

INTRODUCTION

Breaking Our Chains

Dr. Martin Luther King, Jr. breaking chains by linking arms

The tightest chains that bind us are those that we place upon ourselves. We have bound ourselves with war and poverty by accepting the claims of those who tell us that "war and poverty are inevitable," that they are "part of human nature."[1] But that's changing. We are in the midst of a turning point for humanity—a span of 100 years when we are casting off the chains of this narrow-minded view and turning toward peace and prosperity. This turn is not wishful thinking: it is a social movement at a historical time when humanity has an unprecedented opportunity to prevent future wars, eliminate poverty, and create the conditions necessary for a sustainable existence on our planet. These ends can be achieved through a written agreement to live together that is enforceable in the courts of all countries. 2048 is a plan to make this happen.

This movement began with the creation of the Universal Declaration of Human Rights, a set of fundamental human rights for all people, which was adopted unanimously in 1948 by all countries in the United Nations. (The Universal Declaration is attached as Resource A.) My aim with this book is to tell how this movement can be completed in two steps by the year 2048, the 100th anniversary of the Universal Declaration: first, by educating *all* people, including students, in *all* countries about the human rights they *all* share through the circulation of this book and other materials; and second, by drafting a document, an International Bill of Rights, which embodies humanity's agreement to live together and which is enforceable in the courts of all countries.[2] This document is called an International Convention on Human Rights because a convention is a treaty that can be agreed to by all countries. (The draft of the International Convention on Human Rights is attached as Resource B). Throughout this book the terms "International Convention on Human Rights" and "International Bill of Rights" will be used interchangeably.

These two steps, to educate people in all countries while working together to draft an International Convention, are complementary and interrelated. They are good news. The worn-out story that war and poverty are just the way things are so we should keep spending trillions of dollars perpetuating them is giving way to a new story, a new narrative that says peace and prosperity are attainable if we have a plan (which is outlined in this book) and we are willing to challenge those who keep propagating the same old myths.

These may seem like bold claims, and they are, but these changes do not have to happen overnight. 2048 is a *gradual* process that leads to deep-rooted social change. A gradual process is superior to the limited success of sudden violent revolutions. Often violent revolutions only lead to new equally bad rulers with little long-lasting social improvement.[3] Some who are impatient or unable to look beyond their own lifetimes may think planning for enforceable rights by the year 2048 will take too long—but history shows us that truly historic transformations do not happen in leaps, but in turns.[4] That is why 2048 is worth your time.

As you read through this book there are three things to keep in mind:

First, the 2048 movement has been underway for sixty years and is now coming to fruition. As you will see from the introduction and the first two chapters, we are not starting from scratch. The horrors of World War II were the turning point, and many individuals, nongovernmental organizations, universities, businesses (both for-profit and nonprofit), governments, and philanthropic foundations have collaborated to build this movement.

As a result of this work, there is an effective transnational model to follow that is working today for 47 countries in Europe that have ratified the European Convention on Human Rights. The European Convention was the next document to follow the Universal Declaration of Human Rights. It was created in 1950, and works remarkably well for countries as diverse as Russia, the United Kingdom, Romania, France, Turkey, and the Netherlands. Based on this document, and the European Court of Human Rights that enforces it, European countries now live in greater peace and prosperity than they have in centuries. The success of the European Convention demonstrates to the rest of the world the potential for a new social order based on the rule of law rather than the rule of force. *What works for 47 countries in Europe will work for the 192 countries on this planet.* Just as the threat of war has been drastically reduced in Europe, it can be reduced internationally.

Second, 2048 includes every single person, village, town, city, state, and nation. It discards the myth that "me" and "we" are incompatible. When someone lights their candle from yours, they gain light while taking none. Reaching an agreement to live together makes each of our lives better, while also improving the lives of others throughout our international community. With the encouragement of my publisher, I tell parts of my own story in this book as a back story, but that's all it is—a back story, and it's not unique to me. There are many people with similar stories all over the world.

The real story is a collective one; it is about our shared humanity. Despite all the forces pitting us against one another and chalking it up to human nature, the truth is that humanity wants to live as a family and is working to that end. Today there are over one million nonprofits internationally working on social justice issues.[5] The issue is not whether there is enough energy and funding; it is whether we can direct our energy and money into working on something together.

Does widespread participation in 2048 mean that everyone will be happy all the time without any disagreements? Of course not. Show me a family like that and it's probably on television, not in real life. But just as families learn to work things out, so can our human family. To this end, Chapters 3 through 8 lay out the essence of humanity's agreement to live together: "Five Freedoms," to which all people are entitled. By recognizing these rights for all people, they are preserved for each of us.

Third, when you read this book and participate in the 2048 process, it will change your life, and the lives of your children and their children. This is not an overstatement. The enforceable International Bill of Rights that is achieved through the 2048 process affects every major decision and every moment of our lives—including what we can say about a corrupt politician to root out dishonesty, whether we can have a medical operation we need, how we can practice religion, and whether there is a place for us and our children at the university—as well as many other things. The reason 2048 provides a genuine direct impact on each of our lives is that the end result of 2048 not only creates our agreement to live together, but puts that agreement into the hands of judges with strong, impartial courts and institutions to ensure that our agreement is enforced. The 2048 plan is grounded in a strong international tradition of entrusting decision making to neutral, respected persons, whether they are tribal mediators or Supreme Court justices.

A strong international judicial structure to enforce humanity's agreement cannot be achieved without deep and broad thinking. Chapters 9 through 15 lay out a concrete process, supported by the infrastructure of the Internet and the affiliation of many universities, nongovernmental organizations, businesses, and philanthropies, for the realization of fundamental human rights on every corner, hillside, plain, and island around the globe. 2048 is a plan.

One of the main reasons I participate in 2048 is that, like so many others, I'm tired of hearing laments from people complaining about circumstances but having no plan to have a significant impact on the scheme of things. 2048 redirects lament into a document that is an enforceable agreement. This agreement is our *social contract,* an understanding about how we will treat and respect one another as well as an understanding with the representatives of government about how they will govern in exchange for our giving them the power to govern. And if elected officials fail to follow our agreement, they will be forced to do so through court orders issued by judges.

By discarding the propaganda and myths of others—most of whom are becoming wealthy or want to preserve their political power—we can break free from the war, poverty, and environmental ruin we are living with daily by maintaining a flawed international social order. Our international community is ready not just to rattle our chains, but to burst them. Through 2048 we can restructure our society to ensure peace, prosperity and a healthy environment; however, we must have the strength to break the chains that bind us.

Fortunately, the Internet makes it easier for us to break our chains by writing humanity's agreement to live together. The 2048 Project at the University of California, Berkeley Law School has been organized to facilitate this international collaboration. Berkeley Law is not the leader of the 2048 Project, it is a *facilitator.* The 2048 Project is an affiliation of universities, human rights centers and institutes, and businesses, both for-profit and nonprofit, which are working together without any hierarchy to further a dialogue about enforceable human rights. The question before us is, can humanity reach an agreement to live together? All participants in 2048 have equal voices in offering answers. We are all in this together.

As discussed in detail in Chapter 14, "Write Together," through its website, www.2048.berkeley.edu, the 2048 Project provides the means for everyone to participate in writing this agreement regardless of political party, race, wealth, education, sex, religion, or any other background that may have been used to divide us from one another in the past. Everyone from every nation and from every walk of life is welcome at the 2048 drafting table. The website is designed so that it is easy for people in all countries to comment about what they think should be included within an International Convention. If someone cannot log on to the Internet, then he or she can write a letter to the 2048 Project at the law school and their comments will be posted on the website.

As we think together about what we can do together (other than to lament), please remember that it's not just a declaration that we are after. The goal is to have a written agreement that is enforceable in the courts of all countries by the year 2048, not merely to start then. Please see the timeline at the beginning of the book, and feel free to refer to it as you proceed through the chapters. The timeline gives us tangible goals and benchmarks. It will take widespread participation to achieve the benchmarks in the timeline. We all bring our thoughts to the marketplace of ideas by making comments on the

2048 website. By making a comment you spark others to do so; we are brainstorming together. This book is short, 50,000 words, so it is easy to read and to share with others, including book groups and on radio or television shows, and it can be easily translated. Please write to me with any suggestions or leads for appearances to help spread the word about the 2048 movement. In addition, the book is a way to raise funds for the website, translation, and other expenses. All proceeds from this book go to the 2048 Project.

Chapters 11 through 15 tell you what actions you can take; what you do with what you read about 2048 is as important as what's written in this book. The success of the plan for peace and prosperity outlined here depends on our willingness to act. As Einstein explained, "The world is a dangerous place to live, not because of the people who are evil, but because of the people who don't do anything about it.[6] Because what you say to others about the book and how you participate in 2048 is important, the last four chapters explain how we can focus, think, write, and decide together to implement the 2048 plan. Using 2048 we can help one another to remove our chains. We are making sure that we are free universally, and not just within a particular country.

Thomas Jefferson, influenced by his experience in France during the French Revolution, understood the universal nature of rights. Fifty years after he wrote the Declaration of Independence, near the end of his life, he wrote that the Declaration was intended to cast off chains for everyone, everywhere: "May it be to the *world* [emphasis added] what I believe it will be to some parts sooner, to others later, but finally to all, the signal of arousing men to burst the chains under which monkish ignorance and superstition had persuaded them to bind themselves..."[7] "Some parts sooner, to others later, but finally to all"—this is the heart of the 2048 Project. The time has come for human rights to apply to all, regardless of the country in which they live. As U.S. President Dwight Eisenhower, supreme commander of Allied forces in World War II, stated, "The people want peace so badly that one of these days government had better get out of their way and let them have it."[8] Today is that day.

The 2048 Project enables us to work together from a single website to restructure our social order in an unprecedented way. Today we can put our computers, cell phones, and anything else that connects us to the Internet on our kitchen tables, and send a comment. As Tim Berners-Lee, the founder of the World Wide Web, which runs on the Internet, recently explained, this new type of international brainstorming is enabling humanity to solve problems such as disease in ways never done before.[9] In particular, our young people today are ready to cross cultures and political divides to solve problems with our social order, but for them to do so effectively they must be taught about the evolution of human rights. *2048* gives students at the high school and university levels the knowledge they need and the means to act.[10]

Today there are many "leaders" in the world and most of them are not in political positions, nor are they only in castles or in large government buildings. Our leaders can be found internationally, in homes, offices, bookstores, construction sites, classrooms, and cafes. And when we turn our collective power to reaching an agreement to live together, we will succeed. There is nothing more powerful than 6.7 billion people thinking, speaking, and writing together. We can turn our social order away from war and poverty and toward peace and prosperity. As President John F. Kennedy said, "Our problems are man-made; therefore they can be solved by man."[11]

Thank you for participating in 2048 by reading this book, telling others about it, commenting on our website, and any other contribution you can make. As you can see, 2048 is an ongoing dialogue. This book is written in a similar vein. Just as there are evolving new versions of the International Bill of Rights being drafted as part of the 2048 process, so too there will be a new edition of this book in response to new insights from readers. If you write to me, I will surely write you back.

Dr. John Kirk Boyd, Esq.
Executive Director, 2048 Project

University of California, Berkeley Law School
2850 Telegraph Ave., Suite 500
Berkeley, CA 94705-7220
kboyd@law.berkeley.edu
www.2048.berkeley.edu

PART ONE

HOW THE 2048 MOVEMENT BEGAN

CHAPTER 1

Turning Point for Humanity

Elie Wiesel speaks for the conscience of humanity

In *Night,* Elie Wiesel wrote this eyewitness account of what he saw as a prisoner at a Nazi concentration camp:

> Not far from us, flames, huge flames, were rising from a ditch. Something was being burned there. A truck drew close and unloaded its hold: small children. Babies! Yes, I did see this with my own eyes ... children thrown into the flames. (Is it any wonder that ever since then, sleep tends to elude me?)[12]

This moment, as the stench of burning human flesh rushed up into his nostrils, was a turning point for humanity. The turn is not yet completed, but here it began. Why was this moment a turning point? Hadn't this type of thing happened before? Yes, of course it had. But it was a turning point because after the despicable acts of the 1930s and 1940s, humanity collectively bound together in 1948 and said, "never again." Humanity decided to create a new system of rules for those who govern, a new agreement that would not allow such acts to happen again. "Never again" was the goal, not only for Jewish people, but for all of humanity.[13]

With the 1948 beginning of a 100-year turn etched in our minds, let's now consider what it will be like at the end of that turn in the year 2048. At the end of the turn, there will be humanity's written agreement to live together embodied in an International Bill of Rights that is enforceable in the courts of all countries. Now that we have a clear beginning and end, the rest of this book will fill in all that has happened since the beginning and all that needs to happen to reach the end.

I have a specific example of how writing our agreement to live together into an enforceable document will work. I began my career after law school at a large law firm, Morrison & Forester, in San Francisco, California. I was trained as a trial lawyer. My mentor is a legendary barrister, James Brosnahan. Jim is the kind of lawyer you can go to no matter what kind of trouble you are having, whether it's with a person, a business, or a government. If someone has done you wrong, no matter how powerful he or she may be, Jim will go to court, talk to a judge or a jury, and make it right.

How does he do this? In the breast pocket of his shirt Jim always carries a copy of the U.S. Constitution. For over fifty years he has used it in courtrooms across the land, including the U.S. Supreme Court, to protect the rights of all people—from a poor Mexican woman who was part of the Sanctuary movement, to a chief executive officer of a major corporation.[14]

Having learned from Jim, I also have my own bound copy of the U.S. Constitution, and I have used it in many courts, including the U.S. Supreme Court. The Bill of Rights in the U.S. Constitution is both a sword and a shield. It empowers people to stand before a judge to obtain an order against government officials to make them do something, or to stop doing something. With the Bill of Rights, Americans—regardless of their race, sex, age, religion, and creed—can enforce their agreement to live together, as well as their agreement with their government.

I have handled many free speech cases. The free speech guarantee in the First Amendment to the U.S. Constitution enables lawyers like me and any other lawyer in America to stop the government when it tries to interfere with people or organizations engaged in free speech. The Bill of Rights also guarantees other freedoms, including the freedom of religion. Our agreement to live together is fully realized because our rights can be enforced in court.

This process, the ability to stand before a judge with a document and obtain an order to protect rights, is at the very heart of the 2048 plan. Human rights are never fully realized unless you can stand before a judge and enforce them. In fact, this process works so well that it has given rise to a movement to make the protection of rights by judges regional and international. Today, lawyers in forty-seven countries in Europe are carrying copies of the European Convention on Human Rights, in their pockets and briefcases, and they are obtaining orders based on that document.

2048 follows this European example, by drafting an International Bill of Rights that applies in all regions of the world. Human rights are universal; therefore they must be enforceable in the courts of all countries. No one should be free from slavery in one country but not another; no one should have the right to education in one country but not another, and no one should have the right to speak out against the government in one country but not another. The question, therefore, is the following: What will be the wording of the document that will eventually be in the pockets of lawyers in all countries? The 2048 Project provides a way for our international community to decide what the wording of the document will be. The enforceable document produced through the 2048 process is the end of the 100-year turn.

Although it will take some time for this International Bill of Rights to be taken out of pockets and briefcases and used in courtrooms all over the world, through 2048 we are preparing for that day. You can see a draft of this International Bill of Rights today by looking at Resource B in the back of this book, and by going to the 2048 website. The existing draft is only a starting point, not a finished document.

It may seem premature to build a document that may not be used for many years, but I think we have a valuable lesson to learn from the South Korean people. While at a meeting of the World Federation of United Nations Associations in Seoul, Korea, I went to visit the Demilitarized Zone. To my amazement I saw a beautiful train station right on the border with North Korea—the Dorasan Station. It is a large and immaculate structure with sweeping contemporary architecture. But no trains arrive and depart from there. South Koreans have built that station based on their determination that one day South and North Korea will be reunited and the trains will come. So it is with the 2048 Project. We will build an International

Bill of Human Rights now and it will be used later. Someday trains will be regularly pulling into Dorasan Station, and an International Bill of Rights will be regularly pulled out in courtrooms in all countries. Both will be happy occasions.

Equally important, the International Bill of Rights that is being written through the 2048 process will not only be pulled out of the breast pockets and briefcases of lawyers, it will also be pulled out of the backpacks and book bags of students in classrooms in all schools in all countries! Joanna Kim works with the 2048 Project. When Joanna was in high school she was a member of a constitution team that debated about the content and application of the U.S. Constitution, including the Bill of Rights. Joanna had a bound version of the U.S. Constitution that she would pull from her backpack and use to argue before teachers, just as Jim Brosnahan pulls the constitution from his breast pocket to argue in court.

When the constitution is pulled out of Jim's pocket or Joanna's backpack it is used as the basis for upholding Americans' agreement to live together. It says, "Here's the deal," and when people from the classroom to the courtroom learn of this agreement, and pull out the Bill of Rights to use it, then it becomes the very fabric of the culture, and it is respected, not only because judges enforce it, but also because those rights become part of everyday life. To this end, the ultimate outcome of

2048 is respect for one another through an understanding about the rights we all share.

So here are the three steps for the entire 100-year turn: First, we write our agreement to live together. Second, we insist that those in power make our agreement enforceable law in exchange for our allowing them to govern. Third, we teach students about our agreement and we go to court to enforce our agreement, because history has shown that even a written agreement may be violated by government officials unless we go to court and obtain orders to stop them. The struggle to maintain rights is ongoing and equal to the struggle to create them.

Looking Back in Order to Go Forward

Now that we have both the beginning and end of the turning point for humanity clearly in mind, let's go back to the beginning in greater detail to give us clarity about how to go forward. As we look back at the horrors of World War II, the starting point was the goal of preventing such atrocities in the future. To fulfill this goal, a list of rights was created. For thousands of years—with sticks, stones, bullets, and bombs—our ancestors have dominated one another through force. At the same time there has been a steady progression of documents that have not been completely effective, but they do represent a gradual evolution toward an alternative to brute force.

This writing process began with Hammurabi's code in Babylon, 1795BCE, and was continued through the Charter of Cyrus, Persia, 539BCE, English Magna Carta, 1215, the American Declaration of Independence, 1776, the French Declaration of the Rights of Man, 1789, and the U.S. Bill of Rights, 1791. After more than fifty million soldiers and civilians were killed in World War II, we collectively said, enough, we will not allow the person with the biggest club or the most powerful gun to ruin and take our lives. We then turned our attention to a new list of rights that embodied four fundamental rights for all people in all countries.

U.S. President Franklin D. Roosevelt created a short list he called the Four Freedoms in his State of the Union address in 1941: Freedom of Speech, Freedom of Religion, Freedom from Want, and Freedom from Fear.[15] The 2048 movement, and all of the forthcoming chapters in this book, are about the genuine realization of these Four Freedoms, along with a new Fifth Freedom that is imperative with our times, Freedom for the Environment.

At the end of the war these Four Freedoms were built into the Charter of the United Nations.[16] Support for the protection of these fundamental rights came from a wide cross-section of international civil society, including nongovernment and government organizations from many countries. Through a cooperative effort among nonprofit groups and government representatives, our international community seized on its ability to put a new agreement into writing so that it could be enforced against those who govern.[17]

This new framework for universal human rights came to life in San Francisco in 1945 as the world joined together to draft the U.N. Charter. Delegates from countries around the globe passed between four giant columns as they streamed into the War Memorial Opera Building for meetings. The four columns represented the foundation of humanity's new agreement to live together. Each column represented one fundamental freedom to which *all* people, in *all* countries, are entitled. President Roosevelt had made it perfectly clear in his speech that these Four Freedoms had to apply "everywhere in the world." The President was so emphatic about the international application that he hand wrote in the words "everywhere in the world" after each freedom. Roosevelt understood that for humanity to make the turn from war to peace we have to turn together.

Unfortunately, President Roosevelt died before the U.N. Charter was completed. However, his list of four fundamental rights lived on. The delegates to the United Nations built in the creation of a new Commission on Human Rights as a core part of the United Nations, and the new U.S. president, Harry Truman, stated at the closing ceremony of the United Nations in San Francisco that "the first task of the new Commission is to draft an International Bill of Rights."[18] The expectation was that a new International Bill of Rights would embody the Four Freedoms for all people. A new agreement was to emerge from the ashes of war! Something was to be gained from all that had been lost.

A new draft of the International Bill of Rights emerged under the leadership of a diverse group of people on the Commission on Human Rights. Eleanor Roosevelt, following in her husband's footsteps and striding on her own, became the chair of the Commission. She worked with René Cassin from France, P.C. Chang from China, Charles Malik from Lebanon, John Humphrey from Canada, and many others, to draft a new document.

While it was understood at the beginning that they were to write an International Bill of Rights, it became apparent that they did not have the political support for a document that could be enforced in courts against governments. The Cold War was a major reason there was a lack of political support for an enforceable International Bill of Rights. As a by-product of the Cold War, the West and the East became polarized with respect to civil and political rights and economic and social rights. Despite the inclusion of both civil and political (e.g., free speech and freedom of religion), and economic and social (e.g., education and health care) rights within the Universal Declaration, fragmentation developed in which civil and political rights were called "first generation," while economic and social rights were supposedly "second generation." This false hierarchy did not reflect the equal status of all rights as intended in the Declaration. One of the main purposes of the 2048 movement is to repair this fragmentation and boost economic and social rights up to the equal status they originally had and which they deserve.

Another reason for the opposition to an enforceable International Bill of Rights was that in 1948 segregation was still part of the law of the United States, and the British empire was still practicing colonialism. While acknowledging the important role that both the United States and Great Britain had in the formation of the Universal Declaration and the emergence of human rights after World War II, it is also necessary to accept that there were strong forces of dominance and prejudice in those countries. U.S. Senators from the South, for example, did not want an enforceable International Bill of Rights that would make them eliminate segregation because they resisted the notion that equality was a fundamental right. This historical blemish is another reason that we should be working for enforceable human rights.[19]

Given the strong opposition to an enforceable Bill of Rights, Eleanor and others, not wanting the entire agreement to fail, took the wise step of drafting an unenforceable "declaration" of rights instead of an enforceable International Bill of Rights. It was their belief that a Declaration would still serve the important purpose of putting an agreement into writing. Once in writing, even if it was legally unenforceable, it would have a strong moral force and future documents could be written that would make the rights in a Declaration enforceable in courts of law.[20] The result was the Universal Declaration of Human Rights which was adopted unanimously by all countries on December 10, 1948. This was a brilliant continuation of the turn for humanity. In the aftermath of the slaughter of World War II, a written document emerged with a long list of specific rights for people *everywhere in the world.*

The Four Freedoms were built into the Universal Declaration by including them in the Preamble:

> The advent of a world in which human beings shall enjoy freedom of speech and belief and freedom from fear and want has been proclaimed as the highest aspiration of the common people.

Starting with the Four Freedoms as the "highest aspiration" of the common people was an emphatic statement that the common people were building a new social order that would govern their lives. By putting their rights into a document, the people made it clear to political representatives in government that in exchange for being given the power to govern they must abide by a list of rights to assure a decent life for all people regardless of nationality, profession, caste, sex, and other personal differences.

The framers of the Universal Declaration understood that putting our social contract into writing does not make it immediately enforceable, and they were not so naïve as to think that this would happen. After thousands of years of brutes beating down and shooting people, it was not expected that the brutality would stop overnight with the writing down of rights on paper, and it didn't. The important thing, however, is that even though it was understood to be a long, ongoing process, immediately after World War II, using our ability to read and write (which sets us apart from all other species), people set out to devise a social order—whether it is among nations, or between a man and a woman—in which the club did not prevail. Despite expectations that some individuals and nations would continue to act like brutes, because some always will, the Universal Declaration provided a written framework of human rights for all people in all countries to curb these tendencies. They knew it would take time, but they were confident that the movement would continue and 2048 shows they were right. As Eleanor Roosevelt said at the time, "The future belongs to those who believe in the beauty of their dreams."

Given the inability to create an enforceable document because of the influence of the Cold War, the drafters also built language into the end of the Universal Declaration, Article 28, which prepared the path for future documents to make the rights in the Universal Declaration enforceable in courts of law. Article 28 states, "Everyone is entitled to a social and international order in which the rights and freedoms set forth in this Declaration can be fully realized."

Following this vision of future documents to make the Universal Declaration enforceable, two "twin" covenants, the Covenant on Economic and Social Rights and the Covenant on Civil and Political Rights, were ratified in 1976. These treaties have been signed by many countries and have contributed to the enforceability of the Universal Declaration. These Covenants, however, are riddled with exceptions and the "reports" by countries about the progress they are making are typically whitewashed. In almost all countries these Covenants are not enforceable in courts. The Civil and Political Covenant does have a committee that issues opinions when countries agree to accept these opinions, but the opinions are nonenforceable.

The lack of legal or economic repercussions against states for violations of human rights translates to widespread impunity for human rights violations. Amnesty International and Human Rights Watch are wonderful organizations, but "blame and shame" of governments is no longer enough. These organizations have awakened our human conscience, but now it is time to use that awakening to create legal ramifications for the violation of human rights.

It is not a complete surprise that these Covenants are weak and we are stuck halfway through the turn with reports and unenforceable opinions. One of the foremost authorities on international law, H. Lauterpacht, expressed concern at the time of the passage of the Universal Declaration. He wrote that it was dangerous to pass an unenforceable statement of rights because it would give the impression that it was law, when it was not. In his seminal book, *International Law and Human Rights,* he expressed his reservations by foretelling the problem we now face:

> ...there is nothing in the Declaration adopted by the General Assembly which includes—or implies—any legal limitation upon the freedom of states. It leaves that freedom unimpaired. In that vital respect it marks no advance in the enduring struggle of man against the omnipotence of the State. The moral authority of a pronouncement of this kind cannot be created by affirmations claiming for it such authority.[21]

Despite Lauterpacht's forewarnings, many people today continue to talk about the Universal Declaration as if it is enforceable. We should not continue to recite the Universal Declaration like a mantra with the mistaken impression that somehow enough incantations will make it enforceable in courts. Even worse, constantly teaching children that they have these "rights" when they are unenforceable provokes skepticism among our youth. I once worked with several nonprofit organizations sponsoring a play at a large public high school in San Francisco. The play was performed on "International Human Rights Day," December 10, as part of a celebration of the day that the Universal Declaration of Human Rights was adopted.

With the guidance of professional directing, the students were allowed to write their own play. To my surprise, the play began with students at center stage tearing in half booklets of the Universal Declaration of Human Rights and throwing them down on the stage! Why? Because of the disconnect they felt between the rights listed in the Universal Declaration and the experience of those rights in their daily lives.

They chanted while tearing:

> A right to health care? Then why don't I have any?"
> Equality? Then why aren't women paid the same?"
> Education? Where's my place at the university?"

And who can blame them? The rights in the Universal Declaration have been read to audiences repeatedly (I have heard it many times), but they have yet to be realized.

In addition, hundreds of websites recite the rights in the Universal Declaration until human rights start to sound like fantasy, not reality. Fortunately, as the play progressed, the chanters gradually reclaimed these rights by demanding, and then portraying, the realization of them. What struck me at the time was that these young people viewed rights as something they should *live,* not just *learn* about. These students are a good example for us to follow. Humanity is stuck part way through the turn, and they inspire us to keep on going until the rights in the Universal Declaration are genuinely realized by all people.

2048 helps remedy the greatest deficiency of the Universal Declaration: its lack of enforceability. As

Lauterpacht further stated: "There are no rights unless they are accompanied by remedies."[22] The International Bill of Rights that is being drafted as part of 2048 takes the Universal Declaration, along with important covenants, and combines them into a single document that is enforceable in all courts. This International Bill of Rights creates an International Court of Human Rights to enforce the document so there is always genuine accountability.

In addition to enforcement of the Universal Declaration, there is another important reason for us to prepare an International Bill of Rights today: the process of writing and implementing an International Bill of Rights will ensure genuine consent by all countries. There were only 53 countries in the world when the Universal Declaration was adopted unanimously, today there are 192. These additional 139 countries should be given the opportunity to participate in an international dialogue about the human rights to be included in a new document, rather than just being told that they should go along with the Universal Declaration and that it applies to them as a matter of customary law.

Some supporters of human rights fear opening up such a direct dialogue, but when it comes to a social contract, as with any agreement, it's better to be up front about what is being agreed to. The recent adoption of the Charter of Fundamental Rights for the European Union shows that when the process is opened up even more rights can be created. The new

European Rights Charter includes education and health care as enforceable rights in 27 countries!23 Besides, consent is essential to later enforcement because there will be genuine acceptance rather than the imposition of human rights standards.

It's also valuable to have all countries directly involved because it is *within* those countries where human rights will come to be fully realized. It's important to understand that the 100-year turn does not end at the United Nations—it ends at local courthouses. The International Court of Human Rights created by 2048 is not part of the U.N. system, it is *outside* of the United Nations. The same is true for the European Court of Human Rights; it too is *outside* of the United Nations.

The first place for the enforcement of the International Bill of Rights drafted by 2048 is the *local* courthouses. By the year 2048, human rights should be enforceable in the *local* courthouses of all countries. This is the goal. Whenever human rights are being violated the first stop should be the local courthouse. Where necessary, the international community should invest in improving inadequate facilities and compensating underpaid judges.

This is the approach that is used for the European Convention on Human Rights; it first applies in the local courts of all 47 European countries before the cases ever go up to the European Court of Human Rights. The application of the International Bill of Rights in the 2048 plan is what separates it from so many other aspirational statements. The 2048 International Bill of Rights is more than another statement of hope for rights, or a declaration of rosy intentions. It does more than require countries to fill out some reports in which they halfheartedly claim they are making progress toward realizing rights. Humanity has enough of those. Such statements are an insufficient social contract and no longer reflect the extent of our ability to read, write, and communicate with one another to create a just contract among ourselves and with those who govern. Today we can do better.[24]

Just because an International Bill of Rights and the court that enforces it are designed to be outside of the United Nations does not mean that the United Nations does not have an important role to help complete the turn. To the contrary, as we have seen through our discussion of the U.N. Charter and the Commission on Human Rights that drafted the Universal Declaration, there is important work for the United Nations to do. The Human Rights Council, the successor to the Commission on Human Rights that drafted the Universal Declaration, should join in this work. The primary reason we now have an international social movement to complete the turn by the year 2048 is that thousands of organizations and individuals have dedicated their lives, and their funds, to steadily building up human rights so they now have become part of the thinking and expectations of people throughout the world.

Much of this has been done through the United Nations.

However, while the Human Rights Council should be involved, we must also be realistic and accept as fact that the Council cannot be counted on to act on its own to make the rights in the Universal Declaration legally enforceable. Many representatives of the national delegations at the Council have forgotten their power is derived from the people they represent, or they have little flexibility because they are tightly controlled by their governments. Too often the rest of us have accepted the role of begging for changes to be made to our social order rather than exercising our power to restructure and rebuild that order. The only way that we will complete the turn and the rights in the Universal Declaration will become legally enforceable in all countries is by creating an international social movement that demands it, not by patiently asking governments to act. This highlights a major difference between 2048 and most human rights efforts—while governmental representatives are welcome, 2048 is not asking them for permission. 2048 is an international movement *outside* of government; it is the people of all countries thinking and writing together to reach their own agreement that governments must implement. This is what has happened with the Charter of Fundamental Rights for the European Union, and it will happen for the rest of the world as well.

From time to time we must lead our leaders, or accept the domination of special interests who lead them when we shirk our responsibility. It's not sacrilegious to acknowledge the deficiencies in the Universal Declaration and to act together to correct them. Even Eleanor Roosevelt noted in her journal on the night of the passage of the Universal Declaration, December 10, 1948—a date that I celebrate with others every year—that she wondered how valuable it would be to have a declaration that was unenforceable.[25]

The answer to Eleanor's contemplation is that the Declaration has been invaluable. Without the Universal Declaration we would not be partly through the turn. Thanks to this start we can now convert the Declaration into law. As former U.S. Vice President Al Gore recently said, "It's important to change light bulbs, but it's more important to change the law."[26] Whether it is enforceable law to prevent climate change, or enforceable law to ensure the equality of women, the law is not going to change sufficiently unless it rewritten by the people, not governments. Al Gore is not the first leader to stress that it is up to the people to act to change the law. Thomas Jefferson said, "Every government degenerates when trusted to the rulers of the people alone ... the people themselves therefore are its only safe depositories."[27]

This quid pro quo, an exchange of one thing for another—in this case a list of rights in exchange for the power to govern—is not difficult to understand. If you think about our daily lives; we do it all the time. In business we make agreements, "I'll let you use the land, but there are limits on how you may use it." Or with our children, "OK, you can go out, but there are limits on what you can do and you had better follow them." It is the same for government. We, the citizens of all countries, allow those we elect to govern, but there are limits on what they can do and obligations they must fulfill. Such is our undertaking with the 2048 social movement.

It takes a lot of energy to build a house on a foundation, and it will take a lot of energy to build a new, enforceable document on the Universal Declaration and other documents. But we are great builders! We can do anything we set our collective minds to do. This is what the twenty-first century offers us. The challenge is not whether we can complete the turn, it's whether we show up to do the job. Fortunately, *responsibility gravitates to those who accept it,* and people around the world are accepting responsibility by putting their hands and minds together through the 2048 process to draft humanity's agreement to live together. Let us now look at the challenges and opportunities before us to write our agreement to live together and finish this 100-year turning point for humanity.

CHAPTER 2

Challenges and Opportunities

Business leader Robert Haas has called for an international framework for human rights and business

While we have seen that we are partly through the turning point for humanity and how we can complete the turn together, the 2048 movement faces two significant roadblocks: (1) misplaced ego, and (2) an overestimate of the funding required to write and implement humanity's agreement to live together.

Letting Go of Ego

It may surprise you but the biggest impediment to the creation of an International Bill of Rights enforceable in the courts of all countries is not evil leaders; it is ego. It is professors who care more about who is suggesting something than about the idea that is being suggested. It is the leaders of nongovernmental organizations who, despite the fact they are doing similar work, often see other nongovernmental organizations as competitors rather than colleagues. It is media that are more concerned about the celebrity of an organization than about what it is doing. It is business leaders who will not work on an idea unless they thought of it. And it is political figures who care more about driving wedges between peoples and nations to maintain their personal positions of power than about threading together the common interests of our evolving international community.

I personally have no wealth, position or special family lineage. I was born in California and grew up in a middle-class family. My father was an architect and my stepfather a professor. My mother was a schoolteacher and my stepmother a bookkeeper. To the extent that I have any insight or ability to report on what I've found through studying about an agreement for humanity to live together, it is a gift from the people of the State of California who have afforded me a good public education through the

University of California system, first at Santa Barbara as an undergraduate and then at Berkeley for my three law degrees, JD, LLM, and JSD. Although I am one of the people involved in the formation of 2048 as a project, no one person, organization or university can be a "founder" of the natural evolutionary process of humanity toward an agreement to live together. All of us must let go of ego.

I hope that it is also apparent that the strength of 2048 is not any one person or organization, but the idea that we can come to our senses and use our ability to read and write to reach an agreement to live together—something much more enduring than one person's leadership. The views about 2048 that you read in this book are mine alone. Many others may share them, to one degree or another, but I do not speak for the 2048 Project, nor does anyone else. As you will see, a fundamental tenet of the 2048 process is that it is the *weight,* not the *source* of the idea that matters. This is why 2048 actively encourages ideas from all people, even those who challenge the fundamental principles of enforceable human rights. There is no better standard than the one articulated by Jonathan Simon, a Berkeley Law professor and the Principal Investigator for the 2048 Project at the law school: "Whatever people have to say, let them say it, indeed encourage criticism, but let them *put it in writing* so that it may be carefully assessed and responded to in writing." In this way we can pare down ego and weigh the kernel of every idea.

Fortunately, many people are willing to let go of ego. They know they have more to gain if they do. As cellist Yo-Yo Ma has said, "What I look for in musicians is generosity. There is so much to learn from each other and about each other's culture."[28] With this same generous view, 2048 is bringing people together from businesses, the media, universities, scientific communities, nonprofits, foundations, and governments—concerned individuals and experts from every profession and trade, from every country and village—who are willing to look at life and people with open minds and spirits. This type of collaborative social networking as peers, even across professions and age groups, is creating a new "wealth of networks" in society, and 2048 is working in tandem with this movement.[29]

Recognizing ego as an impediment is the first step to removing it. Today, private individuals and political leaders are increasingly setting ego aside and beginning to collaborate together to create a universal framework of enforceable rights through an International Convention on Human Rights. In so doing they are not only carrying on the tradition of support for the Universal Declaration, they are working toward achieving a long-range goal with a definite completion date.

Business and Ego

Thankfully, this trend toward limiting ego is also occurring among nonprofit and for-profit businesses. Too often in the past people in the nonprofit community have looked at themselves as the solution to the problems created by the for-profit sector. Fortunately, those days are ending and a new understanding is emerging. It's not that the people in for-profit businesses are inherently bad; it's because a flawed social order has rewarded unscrupulous behavior (for example, gaining profits from using child labor or despoiling the environment). Many for-profit business leaders understand this and want to change the rules so that there is no business incentive for this type of behavior. The 2048 Project was launched at the Berkeley Law School on Leap Year Day, February 29, 2008. Human rights leader Mary Robinson, former president of Ireland and U.N. High Commissioner for Human Rights, and business leader Robert Haas, former chairman and chief executive officer for Levi Strauss & Co., were the keynote speakers.

In his keynote address, Robert Haas called for a "mandatory international framework for human rights and business." The 2048 Project took his wisdom and built it directly into the mission for the Project: "To draft an enforceable international framework for human rights that can be in place by 2048, the 100th anniversary of the Universal Declaration of Human Rights."

Robert Haas's call to action underscores the need to reward corporations that have adopted codes of conduct and want to spread socially responsible practices. In the current global economy, multinational corporations that have adopted voluntary codes of conduct are finding themselves at a competitive disadvantage with unscrupulous competitors who do not have voluntary codes of conduct. Thousands of companies are producing goods under horrendous conditions both for their employees and for the environment, and they take market share directly from responsible businesses. It's time to create a level playing field for capitalism. The company Levi Strauss and others have an economic incentive to support 2048 and an International Convention enforceable in the courts of all countries because it will force their competitors to compete at their level. Many business leaders want to advance human rights and demonstrate that such actions can yield profits as well as be personally fulfilling.

A good example of this trend is the World Economic Forum held in Davos, Switzerland, each year. The forum brings business leaders from around the world to think together about emerging international business issues, including many issues beyond mere profits. For instance, the Davos Forum has appointed a panel of fifteen experts to help devise an "international legal system." It remains to be seen if these experts will support or resist a new bottom line based on fundamental human rights, but they should be thought of as potential allies in the ongoing movement for enforceable human rights.

Working with multinational corporations ought to be approached similarly to working with governments; that is, they are welcome but their permission is not required for 2048 to proceed. 2048 is about the people writing their own agreement to live together, and the people should not have to go begging to business anymore than they should have to beg their government. Humanity's agreement to live together governs both business and government. Taxpayers have a direct monetary interest in the regulation of business through our written social contract. The recent international financial meltdown, for example, has shown that international regulations, legally enforceable, are necessary in order to maintain stability and to limit the abuse that costs taxpayers hundreds of billions of dollars.

There are similarities between enforcement of financial regulations and enforcement of human rights; both call for global solutions. While there is reason for caution working with business, this is a moment of opportunity. Nonprofits are beginning to see for-profits as allies in reaching similar goals. True, for-profits may be aligning behind an international standard for human rights because it is good for their bottom line, but that's fine as long as the humanitarian goals are accomplished. Let's also not assume that they have only a profit motive. For-profit leaders go home and hug their children just as nonprofit leaders do. Having worked in both sectors over many years, I have not seen any reason for one sector to feel it is morally superior to the other. Again, we need to let go of ego.

Scholars and Ego

While the for-profits are joining with nonprofits, scholars are joining with students and the general public. With respect to students, 2048 uses the drafting of documents to focus scholarly research while simultaneously using its educational curriculum to encourage student participation. This approach gives students genuine involvement and provides faculty with valuable research assistance. The result is that 2048 has become a useful tool both for learning and for drafting documents such as an International Bill of Rights. This mixture of scholarly and student comments and papers allows deeper exploration at universities internationally as to the potential for an International Bill of Rights, as well as a forum to respond to the myriad questions, from the philosophical to the practical, which are raised by such a document.

It also makes sense for scholars to include students because student insights can improve scholarship. Young people today throughout the world have an entirely new perspective. They see boundaries differently. Just as the Internet transcends national boundaries, so do the minds of many of our youth. Many of them are experts at interacting with others throughout the world on the Internet and its social networks, including Facebook, Twitter, and others. The idea that humanity can reach an agreement to live together by drafting an International Convention on the Internet is not foreign to them because many of them have already been involved in some type of transnational dialogue. Moreover, given the global nature of the economy and jobs, motivated students have a genuine interest in participating in 2048 because they realize that 2048 is not just for the benefit of our global community, but also for their personal development. This interconnection of the personal and the global makes the timing right for 2048.

Young people also mine the Internet as a source of knowledge. It is astounding how quickly they can find answers to questions using their quick minds and the Internet. Web 2.0 has not just made information available, but through compilation and commentary, it has also converted that information into knowledge. 2048 contributes to this trend by providing a wealth of information about the Bills of Rights for all countries and regions, and then adding papers, articles and books about this information as a source of ever-expanding knowledge that can be put to good use. Everything from the past is available for us to move forward into the future.[30]

There is also beauty in having multiple disciplines, particularly in the social sciences, focus on and discuss something together. Too often departments such as anthropology, sociology, business, psychology, law and education are located on different floors or separate buildings at universities, and there is little interaction among them. Even worse, sometimes there is polarization rather than collaboration. 2048 is a broad-based movement that offers an opportunity for sharing ideas and collaborating with a common goal. Such collaboration is not sharing solely by way of agreement. It also means sharing through constructive criticism.

When Albert Einstein put forward his theories, people did not reject them offhand (at least most did not). They tested them. The same should be done for an International Bill of Rights. Perhaps it will never produce a final product with mathematical certainty, but it will produce a new social order. Multidisciplinary scholarship with student involvement will help the movement think through how we can build a decent life for all people in all countries—and it will cost less than the trillions of dollars we now spend to prepare for and engage in war!

Next, along with students, scholars are also working with the general public. An international database of nonprofit organizations has been compiled, and, although it is difficult to fix a specific number because many nonprofits are small organizations, it is estimated that "there may be as many as 10 million nonprofits in the world."[31] Records show there are more than 1.2 million nonprofits in the United States alone.[32] Most of them are trying to fix cracks in our social order. That's a lot of fingers in dikes and many of these nonprofits are ready to design a new dike. The difficulty for them, however, is that they often lack the funds for in-depth research for solutions, and 2048 provides a good opportunity for scholars to work together with the public to design fundamental solutions that can be built into an International Convention.

There is a lot of enthusiasm within the general public. At one retirement community where I spoke, 300 people gathered to discuss 2048 and gave a standing ovation—not for me, but for Eleanor Roosevelt! Eleanor's dream was to realize the rights in the Universal Declaration for all people in all countries, and those people giving her a standing ovation are willing to work with scholars if scholars are willing to work with them.

Government and Ego

There is a new generation of leadership in government taking hold internationally. President Obama is only one of several new leaders with a deep concern for fundamental human rights. Also, the recent move of the United States to resume its seat on the Human Rights Council, the offspring of the Commission on Human Rights that was chaired by Eleanor Roosevelt, is an indication that the United States is reintegrating within the world community. This new generation of leaders is unafraid to question old assumptions. Many of them either personally questioned authority, including the government's authority to make war or damage the environment, or they can recall hearing stories and seeing the actions of others with whom they can relate. These people do not want to overthrow governments; neither does 2048. Rather, they see government institutions (such as courts) as integral to a good and fair life for all. In addition, many of them have children, as I do, and want to take far-reaching steps to solve social and environmental ills rather than leave them for our children to inherit.

Does this mean that governments are suddenly willing to drop their militaristic approaches to one another? No, not yet. Momentum to prepare for war remains one of our greatest challenges. But the realignment of government leadership gives us an opportunity to forge new alliances. Our international community does not need to agree on everything for us to reach an agreement to live together! What is most important is that we put our thoughts in writing, not that we agree about everything that we write. We need to test disagreements to see if they rest on the inertia of invalid assumptions. It is difficult to know if we agree or disagree until we put our positions and understandings in writing. Of course, when we put our positions in writing there will be disagreements, which should be sought out and addressed, not avoided. Let disagreement ring! But let it be factual, not based on outdated stereotypes and faulty assumptions, and let the public read and respond to it.

The release of ego by business, scholars, and government results in a new air of openness and collaboration. We should feel free to disagree, but let us address the idea, not attack the person. It's petty and weak to attack people personally because they have a new idea, or to assert that they don't know what they are talking about; that's the refuge for tyrants past and present. 2048 relies on a marketplace of ideas, so let's drop the ego and add to the market! Unlike a painting that may be better suited to the work of one person, drafting the future of human rights for all people is better accomplished through universal participation and a free exchange of ideas, both in agreement and disagreement.

The "1%" Solution for Funding

The second challenge to an agreement to live together is funding. There is a misperception that there is not enough funding to bring about the realization of fundamental human rights for all people in all countries. 2048 counters this misperception with what it calls "the 1% Solution." There are two aspects to the 1% solution. First, there is the need for 1% of humanity to take the steps outlined in this book to write an agreement to live together. Second, there is a need to redirect 1% of the gross national product of each country toward the enforcement and implementation of humanity's agreement to live together. In other words, we need 1% to reach the agreement and 1% to fund the implementation of that agreement.

1% TRAVELING UPSTREAM

There is a tendency today for people and organizations to focus on short-term immediate problems rather than long-term solutions. For most of us, myself included, faced with a long-term project like 2048, the first impulse is to look away and focus on what is present. We can quickly discard the hard work of changing our social order by rationalizing that recycling cans and paper and sending funds to an organization that feeds people are more urgent needs, and this is true. However, as Confucius taught, "He who does not look at what is distant will find sorrow near at hand."[33] Climate change is a good example where our individual acts alone will not keep us from finding sorrow near at hand; we need a social movement.

The following story captures this message:

> One day many bodies came floating down a river and into a town. Some were dead, and some seriously hurt. The people in the town were compassionate. They saved those they could, and when the bodies kept coming they set up a hospital and institutions to care for people. Then one day, as they were pulling another body out of the water, someone looked up and said, 'Of course, we should continue to help the bodies coming

> down the river ... but shouldn't we also go take a look upstream?'[34]

2048 provides a path for 1% of humanity to go upstream. This is not to say that we should stop pulling bodies out of the river. Quite the contrary, we must not stop! We should, however, also take a look upstream—even if it is only 1% of us who go upstream while the other 99 percent stay by the river pulling out bodies. If we do not go upstream, then we are institutionalizing the existing flawed social order and perpetuating the flow of bodies down the river. We may sponsor lots of fund-raising dinners and give out many awards to those pulling bodies out of the river, but if this is all we do, then we become culpable by not really dealing with the roots of the problem.

Taking the path upstream together will lead us to a written agreement for humanity to live together. Of course, it's not easy to break our pattern and spend some of our time and funds to head upstream. But think for a moment about the many news articles and television stories reporting human rights abuses that have shaken you. For how long must we endure images of malnourished children and adults suffering from illness and degradation from extreme poverty followed by some tearful person asking us to send more money? Is there any end? Are we going to watch these horrors forever and only send protest letters, bags of rice, and mosquito nets? Is this the best we can do? We should not stop these generous acts, but it is time to do more.

Now is the time, as an international community, to go upstream and address the causes of war and poverty, the major sources of bodies in the river. Looking upstream we can see that we have not followed Roosevelt's lead. We have not brought about the realization of the Four Freedoms everywhere in the world. But now we can. There is an alignment of events that makes this moment in history ripe for 2048. In the United States, the fatigue of war in Iraq, with its death, maiming, and $2 trillion cost, has filled the national psyche with a yearning for peace. In addition, global warming has infused people from every country with a profound and united sense that we have squandered our ecosystem, and the massive international financial meltdown has shown that we cannot let people run markets like pirates who leave the bill for the rest of us to pay.

Fortunately, the 1% solution also applies to philanthropic giving. It will take only 1% of giving to fund the journey upstream. Internationally, philanthropies gave over $100 billion in 2007.[35] One percent can create a successful social movement that will make the year 2048 a historic year. I'm not suggesting that the entire 1% should go to 2048, but 1% of giving should go toward the trip upstream. Margaret Mead's sage advice, "never underestimate the ability of a small group of dedicated people to change the world," applies to foundations and philanthropic giving as well. A small dedicated group of philanthropists can change the world—if they have a plan—and 2048 provides one.[36]

Even better, there are many within the foundation community who are heading upstream, including the Bill and Melinda Gates Foundation, Bono's One Campaign, and George Soros's Open Society Institute, to name a few. They recognize that our international community cannot always be relying on the next billionaire to come along and pull more bodies out of the river. As Melinda Gates, cofounder with her husband Bill of the largest international foundation, told a meeting of thousands of philanthropists, "Yes, it is true we have a lot of money, but it is only a drop in the bucket for what needs to be done." Still, the wealthy few can use their funds to empower the many. Those with resources and exceptional talents can be invaluable by providing the technical expertise and funding so 2048 can proceed upstream and our international community can stem the flow of bodies down the river with an International Bill of Rights.

Once we are upstream, the way to stem the flow of bodies is to build a 1% funding solution directly into the International Bill of Rights document. All countries should be required to contribute 1% of their gross national product (GNP) into a pool of resources to build schools, hospitals, and courthouses. The millennium development goals that countries agreed to at the turn of the twenty-first century should not be "goals" like those of the Universal

Declaration, which are not legally enforceable and are not being met. One percent of GNP for all countries is approximately $500 billion a year. No group of individuals or philanthropic organizations is able to sustain this level of annual giving. It is possible, however, for them to lead and inspire governments to adopt a framework to accomplish this goal. Through their insight, acumen, and funding, businesses and philanthropies can be instrumental in bringing about a 1% solution.

As we consider a 1% solution it is important to recognize that the necessary core of people and organizations exists now, and it's just a matter of bringing them together. It's a matter of using 1% of existing philanthropy to find the 1% of people throughout the world who already share a genuine interest in a new agreement to live together based on human rights. 2048 is a facilitator to bring these people, organizations, and governments together. When people find out about 2048—whether it is through this book, by surfing the Web, or by word of mouth—they often pick up a pen or a keyboard, the tools needed to draft our written agreement to live together. The key is that people *know* there is a movement underway.

One of the reasons people pick up that pen or keyboard is because it is personally rewarding. Eleanor Roosevelt talked about how fulfilling it is to work on human rights, and I see it daily with the people from different backgrounds and countries who are working on 2048. These good feelings are essential for a healthy society. Through participation in 2048, people come to see the law as something other than an oppressive force that is imposed on them. When law emanates from the people they more readily abide by it, both with their government and with one another.

Sure, it's not easy to let go of ego and direct 1% of funding to go upstream. But it is worth it. 2048 enables us to achieve collectively that which we cannot achieve alone. 2048 is a collective effort that no one government can deny. No matter how strongly the government in China states there is no right to free speech, or the government of the United States says there is no right to health care, the people simply will not tolerate this abridgement of the rights set forth in the Universal Declaration any longer. Whether governments like it or not, it is time to draft together an International Convention on Human Rights that will strengthen existing regional courts, create new regional courts where there are none, and harmonize them with an international court so that fundamental human rights will be enforceable in the courts of all countries.

Yes, we are audacious at the 2048 Project, but are we any more audacious than those who tell us that we must accept the destruction of our entire planet's ecosystem through global warming just because we need to compete with one another to make a living? Or those who, despite the tremendous wealth of this planet, perpetuate an international system with huge pockets of poverty from which crime, fundamentalism, and fascism inevitably sprout? 2048 is for those with enough fortitude and leadership that they want to steer their own lives instead of only relying on others to steer for them. It is for those who believe that the people are the leaders, not followers or beggars. And it is for those who dare to rewrite the rules for those who govern, rather than just to wait and hope that politicians and corporations will change their ways when they have a vested interest in the status quo. Millions of people want change. They see opportunities as well as challenges and are ready to work diligently on an agreement to live together.

We turn now to map out in more detail the five core components of an agreement to live together. We do so with confidence despite the challenges we face. "Yes we can" is not just an American political campaign slogan; it is the theme for the twenty-first century. Having made our way through the wasteland of war, we can travel the path less traveled toward peace and prosperity.

PART TWO

WHAT THE 2048 MOVEMENT IS

CHAPTER 3

Five Freedoms for All

President Franklin Roosevelt giving his Four Freedoms speech before the U.S. Congress in 1941

One of the most pernicious myths is that peace and prosperity are hopelessly complicated and unattainable. 2048 dispels myths. This is untrue.

Peace and prosperity can be attained through the realization of five basic fundamental freedoms, for all people, everywhere in the world. They are: freedom of speech, freedom of religion, freedom from want, freedom for the environment, and freedom from fear. Of course, other rights are needed too, but these five fundamental freedoms establish a framework within which other rights can flourish. If our international community remembers these Five Freedoms, and if they become a regular part of our daily lives, then collectively we will carry the core of 2048 in our minds and they will become our way of life.

Please look at your hand for a moment. Hold it up, palm facing you. We all have five fingers, but the first we call a thumb. In appearance it looks different. It stands out. And it is strong. It represents freedom of speech, the idea that stands out, that stands up to dishonesty and corruption. Next, look at your index finger. We point with this one. It gives us direction. It represents freedom of religion. Each of us is free to choose our own direction, with or without God, and for those who decide that God is their guide, then they are free to have their own relationship with God without the state telling them what that relationship must be. Interference by the state pollutes the relationship with God. Third is the middle finger, the longest of all. It represents freedom from want, the long road of existence, and the certainty that there will be food, water, shelter, education, and health care for every one of us no matter where we may be on that road. Next, for many of us, is the marriage ring finger, either the right or the left hand, and for all of us, a finger with a direct link to our nervous system. It represents freedom for the environment. Life. We all have a direct link to the Earth and the ecosystem of which we are a part. When the life of the Earth is spoiled, our lives are spoiled. Finally, there is our "little finger," shorter and smaller than the rest. It represents freedom from fear. It's the "finale" of our hand, our reward. All the others lead to this one.

As you take a look at your hand and recount the Five Freedoms, remember that you didn't ask for that hand, you were born with it. So too, you do not have to ask for the Five Freedoms, you were born with them. They are five freedoms for all!

Four of these Five Freedoms originated with U.S. President Franklin Roosevelt. He stated the following in his State of the Union address to the U.S. Congress in January 1941:

> We look forward to a world founded upon four essential human freedoms:
>
> The first is freedom of speech and expression—*everywhere in the world.*
>
> The second is freedom of every person to worship God in his own way—*everywhere in the world.*
>
> The third is freedom from want—*everywhere in the world.*

> The fourth is freedom from fear—*everywhere in the world.*

The beauty of these Four Freedoms is that they are an outline of an agreement for humanity. The Four Freedoms are a social formula. When we, the people of our international community, have created a social order whereby all people enjoy the first three freedoms—freedom of speech, freedom of religion, and freedom from want—then we will have created a society where we can all share in the fourth freedom, freedom from fear. This formula was born out of a desire not just to end World War II, but as President Roosevelt said "to end the beginning of all wars." This quote and the Four Freedoms are engraved in granite at the Roosevelt Memorial in Washington, D.C. They are a guiding light for 2048.

I recall being at the Roosevelt Memorial in Washington, D.C., at dusk one evening. It is an outdoor memorial with a mix of monuments, trees, and waterfalls. The many cherry trees were in blossom and a light drizzle gilded the petals with water. My friend and I stood before a large stone wall, perhaps 30 feet high, with the Four Freedoms engraved in large letters on it. At that moment a group of twenty-five or thirty middle-school students, 12 to 14 years old, of all different races—black, white, Latino, Asian—came to the wall.

They were from Baton Rouge, Louisiana, United States, but the rights on that wall applied to any visitor from anywhere in the world. The students laughed and formed small groups to have their pictures taken in front of these freedoms. After the flashes stopped, several turned to touch the wall and run their fingers through the carved grooves of the letters on it. The connection for my friend Bart, who is black, and me, white, was clear: It didn't matter what color they were, what sex, what religion or what nation they were from—the rights on that wall must become as real in the lives of all people as they are to the fingertips of those children.

Fortunately, we need not wait for the children to grow old for the realization of the Four Freedoms. Roosevelt saw the Four Freedoms as achievable within a generation. Commenting on his speech, he said, "It is no vision of a distant millennium. It is a definite basis for a kind of world attainable in our own time and generation."[37] Perhaps he was overly optimistic about the speed at which the Four Freedoms could be achieved everywhere in the world, but steady, immediate action is the message—not to put these rights off forever.

The Four Freedoms are the essence of a good life for all. They ensure the following: We can think freely, say and write what we want, and peacefully organize to protest; we can have a relationship with a god of our choosing, without interference by the state; we can live with security knowing that education and health care will always be available, regardless of circumstance; and finally we can live in peace, without fear of rampant crime and continuing war. In short, the Four Freedoms are the core of our social contract—our agreement about how we will live together.

President Roosevelt's recitation of the phrase "everywhere in the world" at the end of each freedom is key. He was so adamant about these words that he handwrote them onto the pages of the speech he gave. He made it perfectly clear that the Four Freedoms were not just for Americans. His own speechwriters questioned him about this, saying that Americans wouldn't be much concerned about the people in Java. Roosevelt's response was that Americans had better care because we are all interconnected now. So as we strive for the Four Freedoms, we do so for all members of our international community. Security rests not in the well-being of one nation, but in the well-being of all nations.

In effect, the Four Freedoms were a New Deal for the world. Roosevelt had long been a champion of the common man in America. Through the New Deal in America, Roosevelt took the hard edges off of capitalism. He made sure that working people were not left destitute while wealth and power were consolidated into the hands of a few. With the Four Freedoms, he was expanding his gaze to all men and women, in all nations, to ensure that destitution did not befall anyone, for in destitution he saw the seeds of war. His wife, Eleanor, saw these seeds as well. In 1942 she wrote, "If we really do not mean that after this war we intend to see that people the world over have an opportunity to obtain a satisfactory life, then all we are doing is to prepare for a new war."[38] Recently we have seen the correctness of this insight in Afghanistan, where Osama bin Laden and Al Qaeda have grown from the soil of crushing poverty.

Soon after Roosevelt unveiled the Four Freedoms they were incorporated into a multinational wartime strategy. A superpower summit between Winston Churchill and President Roosevelt was held aboard American and British ships in the Atlantic Ocean, on August 10, 1941, eight months after Roosevelt stated the Four Freedoms in his State of the Union address. Roosevelt summoned great courage and strength to rise up out of his wheelchair and walk across a ship while it was at sea. Each footstep, with crutches, and braces on his legs, was a stride toward a new deal, a new contract, a new agreement for humanity.[39]

The famous Atlantic Charter came out of Roosevelt's meetings with Winston Churchill at sea, and the Four Freedoms were included in that Charter. Like the Four Freedoms speech, the Atlantic Charter was written for everyone. It envisioned a postwar social order "which will afford assurance that all the men in all the lands may live out their lives in freedom from fear and want."[40] The embodiment of the Four Freedoms in the Atlantic Charter was a defining moment for the social contract between government and the common person.

While the Four Freedoms ensure dignity and cover most of our social contract among ourselves and our government, we also need a fifth freedom to preserve our planet, including the ecosystem that provides joy and beauty, and also sustains us: freedom for the environment. Just as our human DNA is 98.5 percent the same for all people in all countries, so too our well-being is intertwined with our physical environment.[41]

Equally important, as we have learned from global warming, the health of our environment affects us all, everywhere, and therefore, as with the first Four Freedoms, freedom for the environment must also apply "everywhere in the world." The demise of our planet's ecosystem teaches us the folly of only working on local environmental issues while dramatic degradation takes place worldwide. I recall a lawsuit in which I represented an environmental group seeking to protect old growth forests. We won that lawsuit, but now, because of global warming, the temperatures are not dropping enough to kill the bugs that are today killing the trees. We can't just protect the environment at the local level and expect to have a clean and healthy environment.

Furthermore, it's time to discard the myth that we must be willing to sacrifice the environment for the sake of economic competition. What is needed is uniform, international regulation of the type that an International Convention would provide. Without an international approach there will always be pressures for some countries to sacrifice the environment to gain market advantage. Capitalism works well, but it also tends to create a race to the bottom when it comes to environmental protection.

Creating a fifth freedom for the environment is also harmonious with the other four freedoms. Often destruction of the environment results from the actions of impoverished people who are struggling to survive, whether by cutting down their local forest to an extent that it does not grow back, for example, or overfishing to where fish stocks do not come back. The lack of the first three freedoms, particularly freedom from want, can thus lead to the destruction of the environment. As we reach an agreement regarding the first Four Freedoms, well-being for all, the result is that the need to sacrifice the environment to survive is reduced. In this way, the Five Freedoms are intertwined and the success of each bolsters the others.

Given the strength and well-being that each of us will gain from five universal freedoms, it is also time to dispel another myth—that there is not enough to go around. We pay dearly for the myth that we can't afford to have health care and education for all, and the myth that environmental protection is too costly. These myths are untrue. For example, studies have conclusively shown that not only will global warming cause serious suffering and diminishment of our daily lives, but it will cost us more to pick up the pieces after hurricanes, droughts, and flooding than it will cost to avoid these calamities. Similarly, while education may cost more initially, it creates good jobs to construct schools and results in highly productive workers. The net result of the implementation of 2048 is a financial savings in addition to fulfilling lives.

No Increase In Taxes

Furthermore, securing Five Freedoms for all will not require more taxes! All it will take is the reallocation of existing tax revenues. The real myth is that we must continue the way we are going. Our international community is spending *$1.4 trillion* a year on military expenditures. One percent of GNP for all countries is roughly $500 billion.[42] Therefore, all it would take to bring about the full realization of the Five Freedoms and to usher in a new form of human security would be to reallocate $500 billion of military costs toward the realization of the Five Freedoms. That would leave $900 billion for military, more than enough! The truth is that there is enough funding for the realization of fundamental human rights, including economic and social rights. The problem is those who are presently profiting do not want the public to believe there are sufficient funds for military *and* human rights because they have an interest in maintaining the status quo. It is time for the human rights community to have the strength and daring to band together so that we have the clout to stand up to this narrow-minded view.

One way that myths are perpetuated is by keeping people unaware of the truth. Today, for example, the

United States gives only 0.17 percent, less than one-fifth of 1% of its GNP, to foreign aid, and much of this goes for military purposes, not education and health care. One percent of GNP is not too much to ask, particularly when greater security for ourselves and our children is the result. Just think of the cost if the bird flu or some other pandemic were to arise out of abject poverty in a poor country and then sweep the world, killing tens of millions in all countries and causing utter chaos and financial collapse because goods could no longer be produced and shipped in our global economy. A penny of prevention is worth a pound of cure.

People in the United States, on the whole, like people in all other countries, are fundamentally good and generous souls with whom you can sit and talk at their kitchen tables. Many do not know that their government gives less than one-fifth of 1% to foreign aid and is at the bottom for giving among developed countries. They probably also don't know that the United States spends more on military than all other countries combined.[43] Part of the role of 2048 is to help spread awareness. When people know the truth, they typically support reallocation of resources as part of our agreement to live together, in keeping with their self-interest and morals.

Awareness can be created with a small percentage of people. Just as it will only take 1% of GNP for the realization of education and health care for all, so too it will take only 1% of humanity to share the news of

2048. Word of mouth, spurred by our innate desire to live in peace and security instead of war and want, will spread the word. This 1% of humanity already exists within the arts and media, our nonprofit and for-profit businesses, our places of worship, our universities, and even our governments—now the Internet and 2048 are bringing all these communities together.

Knowledge of the Five Freedoms is essential to achieve this 1% "tipping point" for the success of 2048. Students and the public generally need to be able to recall the Five Freedoms just as easily as they can count the five fingers on their hand. As they learn their rights, they also come to expect them, both from one another and from their governments. What they expect today, they will demand tomorrow. The Five Freedoms are deeply held cultural values that lead to lasting results. Now, with the Five Freedoms for all etched firmly in mind, let us consider each of these freedoms individually.

CHAPTER 4

Freedom of Speech

Nelson Mandela exercising his right to free speech

Freedom of speech is Neda, shot by militia, blood flowing from her eyes and mouth as she died on the streets of Tehran in 2009. It's peaceful protesters being attacked with dogs during the civil rights marches in America in 1965, and it's people in India walking headfirst into club-wielding police in 1930. Freedom of speech is the right to communicate how we honestly feel about something peacefully.

The main opponents of free speech are those who suffer from weakness and insecurity: politicians who are afraid that their corruption will be revealed, families who are afraid of losing their hereditary positions, clergy who are afraid that others might listen to God instead of to them, and businesspeople who are afraid they might lose profits, to name a few. The question that must be asked of these people is, "Do you have so little confidence in your own mind and ideas that you cannot permit others to express theirs?"

Contrary to those who would restrict free speech are those with strong and open minds. They are secure enough to allow a marketplace of ideas. A confident mind will actively seek out ideas that are contrary to one's own thinking because only fools believe their thinking is perfect and cannot be improved. Imagination, ingenuity, and insight are all products of unique thinking that questions existing thinking. Without the ability to think critically and the ability to communicate those thoughts, we become stagnant, or worse, boring. A dull, dimwitted life, dictated by others who claim their power to stifle speech, based on heredity or divine guidance, is a terrible sentence. Many people would rather die than suffer such a life. This is why those who limit speech are doomed to fail—it's just a matter of time, because humans will fight, both nonviolently and violently, to speak their minds. People have an innate yearning for justice, and even if it wanes at times, it is one of the strongest virtues of human character.

Freedom of speech is part of our consciousness.[44] It influences our image of ourselves and the world around us. Where freedom of speech is restricted, there is a prevailing fear that limits inquiry, stifles imagination, and reduces self-confidence, resulting in people with less self-respect and creativity. On the other hand, where freedom of speech is in place, there is inquiry, indeed scrutiny, of elected officials and the decisions and actions they take. There is also innovation and daring, because absence of fear increases the willingness to act and risk, to think and suggest things that have not been said or done before, and to question the status quo with an eye toward improvement. These attributes produce people with self-respect and creativity, and true leadership based on ideas and ingenuity rather than force and position.

Often the "new ideas" spawned by free speech are controversial. Take, for instance, Abraham Lincoln's speech in which he boldly stated that America would not be able to survive as a country that was "half slave and half free."[45] This statement was extremely controversial and received a strong public backlash. The controversy was so great that Lincoln's own advisors cautioned him against making similar statements, yet he made them again.[46] This is free speech, when the unpopular idea eventually becomes the law of the land. Lincoln persevered, and slavery was abolished.

Liberty is not only an idea, it is a way of life. Living in fear of speaking or writing honestly because of possible negative repercussions is not liberty. Liberty includes the right to take our own paths, and freedom of speech is necessary to light our way. Freedom of speech allows us to attain our highest personal development and become what we are meant to be, not what some government official decides we must be.

Freedom of Expression

Let's use a simple test for freedom of expression. Can people anywhere in the world write down on paper what they think of any leader in the world and pass out that paper on any street corner to share their view? If not, a violation of a fundamental human right is occurring. It doesn't matter which country or on which street corner the restriction occurs; freedom of speech is universal. There is no excuse for the bogus claim that some cultures allow it, and others do not. Would anyone say the same of slavery? Is slavery okay if it is a cultural tradition? The enslavement of the mind is as egregious as the enslavement of the body.

2048 is itself part of this test. 2048 does not support violence of any kind. To the contrary, 2048 follows Gandhi's path of active nonviolence. This is the same path that was taken by hundreds of thousands of people sweeping into Red Square in Moscow just prior to the downfall of the Soviet Union. It's the path that was taken in the Philippines when the military refused to fire on peaceful protesters and

President Marcos was forced from power, and it's the path that was taken in South Africa where apartheid came crumbling down and Nelson Mandela walked out of the rubble to become president.

Violence is unnecessary because the power of an idea is irrepressible. There may be those who attempt to stop the distribution of this book, but they will never stop the circulation of the idea that humanity can, and will, reach a written agreement to live together. Perhaps humanity's thinking and sharing through the Internet's social networking can still be curtailed, but it is becoming so ubiquitous that it can't be contained. We live in an age in which ideas are circulating around the world at unprecedented speed. No one can control them; no barriers can stop them.[47] The Internet is a healthy example of modern-day free speech and it is also providing an important check on government. This brings us to the second important aspect of freedom of speech; the power to disseminate an idea.

Freedom of the Media

Often we think of the power to disseminate ideas through the lens of freedom of the press, but today it is much more than that—it's the freedom of the airwaves, the cables, the satellites, the Internet, of all means of communication. No government should ever own or control the content of communications. Without an independent media, and all of its manifestations, including the Internet, we lose our guard.

One of the best ways to ensure freedom of speech for our international community would be to protect the Internet so that it can never be dismantled or disrupted by any one government or country. Universal security requires that when the brutes go to pick up clubs someone can alert others and courts can stop them from wielding those clubs.

We must take the steps to guarantee free speech because the struggle for rights only *begins* with a list of rights and the courts to protect them. Free media provide an early warning system at the first indication of the erosion of rights. Having free, worldwide media is the only means by which an independent judiciary can effectively withstand government forces when those governments refuse to abide by the social contract embodied in an international convention. Even after an International Convention on Human Rights has been written and becomes law, the struggle for rights is not over—it never is. It takes as much struggle to preserve rights as it does to create them. Free and vibrant media are always at the vanguard of this continuing struggle.

While empowerment through the Internet is essential, freedom of speech also protects the right of anyone to hand out a pamphlet or some other piece of writing, or to speak on the radio, on television, and at a university or a town meeting. As everyone knows, communication, even when words are involved, includes body language and sincerity. Humans read and process emotions before they even get to the words exchanged. Sometimes there is no better way to relate to another person than to look him or her in the eye in a genuine, nonthreatening way, and hand him or her a piece of writing. The founding fathers of the U.S. government—Madison, Hamilton, Franklin, and Paine—all distributed their thoughts this way.

Unfortunately, for several years now, many governments have been imposing more and more restrictions on pamphlet dissemination. It is not uncommon for government officials to lock people trying to pass out materials behind steel fences like livestock so they can only wave and beg to people from afar. The appearance is that people engaged in free speech are already in prison. Their placement in a pen makes a powerful statement that contaminates both the acceptance of the material and the assessment of its content by the people they hope to reach. Unless there is convincing evidence showing a security risk or a great physical harm, freedom of speech includes being able to hand a pamphlet to people so that they can connect freely with an idea.

Freedom of Assembly

Freedom of speech also includes the right to gather as a group. Freedom of assembly enables us to convey our thoughts with our bodies and our presence, as well as our minds. For many of us, participation in freedom of assembly has influenced our personal lives. Once experienced it is rarely forgotten.

I remember when I was 10 years old and I lived in a small apartment with just my mother. The apartment was across the street from a grocery store, and the assistant manager lived with his wife in the apartment next to ours. Although I wasn't a real employee, I would hang out at the store, and do little things like help straighten up the boxes on the aisles. I got to know the employees at the store, including a guy who was drafted to fight in the Vietnam War. While I don't recall the specifics, I do remember that there were differing views about whether he should or should not go.

Well, he did go. After being there only a short while he stepped on a land mine that blew off his legs and killed him. That's when I learned what a "body bag" was; that's when I started drawing peace signs and attending assemblies at Stanford University to protest the war. Throughout my career arguing civil rights cases, including the right to free speech and assembly, at all levels of courts, I've never forgotten those early experiences. And now I'm working on an International Bill of Rights because I am determined to help decrease the number of body bags in the future, including the possibility my own children could be among them.

Freedom of Association

Finally, there is the right to freedom of association: the right to associate with people we choose and to have those associations free from government prying and interference. Freedom of association also includes the right to vote for those who will lead us, rather than being told who they will be.

First, with respect to the right to decide with whom we will associate, there is no more personal or important decision than whom we will marry. This is a decision that any two people, and no one else, can make. The government has no right to tell us how to choose our thoughts, and it has no more right to tell us how to choose our spouse. Similarly, government has no place telling us how we shall associate with that spouse within the privacy of our bedrooms, including what kind of intimate relations we have.

Second, as long as we gather in a nonviolent manner, and do not espouse killing or other violent acts against people solely because of their race, sex, religion, or some other personal attribute, we have the right to form groups or associations, including political parties. This includes the right to band together to exercise our collective will to support candidates whom we choose to represent us.

Third, through the exercise of our free speech, and as a product of our associations, we have the right to elect those who will represent us. As one of the Five Freedoms, freedom of speech embodies democracy because it ensures that our voices will truly be heard. It also ensures that if those elected do not abide by our agreement to live together, then we can replace them. They should know that they are always one election away from being removed.

In conclusion, my short statement about free speech is itself a good example of free speech. Of course, there are those who will agree or disagree with my views. To them I say, "Put it in writing," just as I have. Then we can have a dialogue to see if we can find common ground. The real gift of free speech is to listen for new thoughts. Of course, we will not always agree, but we should not assume that because we may disagree on one thing that we must disagree about everything. Free speech allows us to take our own path and, through discussions with others on their paths, to find our way together.

Now let's turn to the second of the Five Freedoms, freedom of religion.

CHAPTER 5

Freedom of Religion

Gandhi weaving a common thread of religious freedom

Freedom of religion is our personal belief—whether Muslim, Hindu, Buddhist, Christian, Jewish or other—and it also includes the right not to have any particular belief. The strongest relationship with God, when people choose to have one, is voluntary, not required by the state or by religious leaders. Freedom of religion ensures that the state will stay out of our personal relationship with God so that it may be as strong and genuine as possible. No one should be forced to come to God, nor should anyone be threatened with repercussions if he or she chooses to leave.

Love and commitment for God emanate from the soul, not from coercion.

Speaking for myself, I could not do the work I do on 2048, or write this book, without a deep, abiding faith in God. Rejection, derision, ostracism, and penury have most often been the rewards I have received for the pursuit of this work over ten years.[48] I don't claim that 2048 is "God's plan," nor do I even know exactly what God's plan is. However, I do not believe that God's plan is spending the bulk of our time and money amassing and using weapons, nor do I believe that an international social order that provides a small percentage of people with incredible abundance while two-thirds of the people live in poverty, and often in misery, is God's plan. God did not create us to be harmonious, but we do have the ability to love as deeply as we hate, and to reason and write so that it's possible to craft an agreement to live together.

Freedom of Religious Belief

Let me be clear that 2048 is not a religious movement. 2048 does not favor any particular religion, but some aspects of 2048, such as caring for the sick by recognizing health care as a human right "everywhere in the world," may indeed further God's plan for humanity. I think so, but as I have said before, I do not speak for all of 2048: this is my personal opinion. All religious (and nonreligious) organizations are invited to participate in 2048;

indeed, they are encouraged to do so. As I also explained earlier, the standard of measure for participating in 2048 is the weight of the idea and not who or which organization offers the idea.

I also am sharing my thoughts about my faith in a spirit of openness and tolerance. I don't usually wear my religious beliefs on my sleeve, but in addition to it being the way I genuinely feel, I don't think I can provide a better example of freedom of religion. I can have my own beliefs, and I can share them freely with you. Nobody, including religious leaders or government officials, has the right to punish me for what I believe, or interfere with my sharing my belief with you. This is the essence of religious freedom.

Does this mean that freedom of religion is the rejection of religious teachings or insights of religious leaders? No, I have found excellent guidance from religious leaders. All their advice, however, is only guidance. They are human, and through 2048 they may offer their insights, but they cannot compel us to believe them or to accept that only through them can we communicate with God. We, as individual humans, and as cultures and groups, have different ways of communicating with God, and this is why tolerance is at the core of freedom of religion. Tolerance includes respect for all of our different ways of communicating with God. We are tolerant of others so they will be tolerant of us. We can all have a personal connection with God, or no connection at all, on our own terms, not on the terms dictated by any person or government.

Just because our international community may practice different religious beliefs and have different relationships with God does not mean that we should assume we have little in common. It is a mistake to assume that with respect to religion there is more that is different than what is shared. As part of the research into whether freedom of religion should be included in the Universal Declaration of Human Rights, Eleanor Roosevelt asked Gandhi to research the extent to which there was international support among all religions for freedom of religion. As was his way, Gandhi took the task seriously and studied the question. He then wrote to Eleanor Roosevelt stating, "I expected that the deeper I went, the more disparity I would find. Fortunately, however, the deeper I went the more I found in common." Gandhi's letter suggests that there is a "common thread" that weaves through religious beliefs. This common thread is contrary to much of the dogma today that pits religion against religion and group against group.

Separation of Religion and the State

The key to separation of religion and state is government staying out of religious practices and religion staying out of government activity. The problem arises when government passes laws to make everyone adhere to a particular belief or practice. Take, for example, the consumption of alcohol, which is not in keeping with certain religious beliefs. People should be able to choose freely whether or not to drink. It should not be up to the government to pass a law that prohibits drinking in order to ensure adherence to particular religious beliefs.

Separation of religion and state also prevents government from coercing people to pay to support particular religious institutions. Governments operate with the funds they collect from their citizens. Given that the citizens have differing religious beliefs, government cannot spend funds to support any particular religion over another. Once again, such forced action interferes with the voluntariness of one's relationship with God. If people's beliefs motivate them to give money to a religious institution to build a mosque, synagogue, church, or temple, that's their choice. At no time should they be compelled to fund, through taxes, religious institutions with which they do not wish to be associated.

Having clarified that our strongest relationship with God should be a voluntary one, and that the state should stay out of that relationship so as not to weaken it, let us now turn to the third of the Five Freedoms, freedom from want.

CHAPTER 6

Freedom from Want

Mother Teresa answering the call for freedom from want

Freedom from want is security. This means that despite life's inevitable ups and downs there is a bottom beneath which none of us can fall. Every life has its share of failure along with success. Every life has pain. It's perfectly natural that we desire to create a society that will care for us in the down cycles of life. We need family to help in difficult times, and not just our immediate family, but our human family. Not every personal family has a heart surgeon to perform a needed operation, and not every family has an expert on grammar who will teach others to write. But in our human family we have experts on many things, and we are smart enough to train people with specialties so that they can help others.

Just as we build roads to travel that all of us may use, we also build institutions, schools, and hospitals to ensure that no matter whether we are rich or poor we will always have access to education and health care. In this way everyone has the security of a decent path through life, including a fair chance to contribute to our global economic marketplace.

President Roosevelt described the details of the rights included within freedom from want in his State of the Union speech on January 11, 1944. This speech is known as his "Second Bill of Rights" speech. In it, he provided a list of rights that are included within freedom from want:

> The right to a useful and remunerative job in the industries, shops or farms or factories of the nation;
>
> The right to earn enough to provide adequate food and clothing and recreation;
>
> The right to every farmer to raise and sell his products at a return which will give him and his family a decent living;
>
> The right of every businessman, large and small, to trade in an atmosphere of freedom from unfair competition and domination by monopolies at home or abroad;
>
> The right of every family to a decent home;
>
> The right to adequate medical care and the opportunity to achieve and enjoy good health;

The right to adequate protection from the economic fears of old age, sickness, accident and unemployment;

The right to a good education.

This list, in sum, describes *dignity.* It is the assurance for each of us, regardless of where we happen to be born, or what family we are born into, that through the trials and tribulations of life, in sickness and in health, we will always have a modicum of dignity. Roosevelt believed that poverty is preventable and morally unacceptable. Security and freedom from want should be seen in this light.[49]

Some may say this sounds like "socialism." Let's debunk that myth. Is it socialism when we collect taxes and build a highway so that people can go to work? Or when we design and fund a mass transit system? Is it socialism to train and pay firefighters to be ready on a moment's notice to jump into their trucks and race to any home on any block to put out a fire, be it the home of a rich family or a poor one? Do the "socialist" police come to our rescue when someone is breaking into our home or robbing us? If we hold hands with our children, and walk with them to public school, as I do, are we taking them to a socialist institution? The answer to all of these questions is *no.* As long as people own the land beneath their homes, and the homes themselves, and businesses own not only the land and buildings, but the products they produce, it is a capitalist state—supported by public services.

Sure we could all pay for our own fire protection and have our own fire departments. But what sense would that make? When the fire at the home of a poor family unable to pay for protection becomes a conflagration consuming many homes, is this a wise or ethical social order? Of course not. And it is the same with crime. Yes, people can gate up their homes and leave large numbers of people in squalor outside, but what happens when they drive outside those gates? Muggings, carjackings, and crimes are often perpetrated by people who feel detached from their own society.

George Bernard Shaw said, "The worst sin toward our fellow creatures is not to hate them, but to be indifferent to them: that's the essence of inhumanity." If we reflect on the situation in the world today, indifference permeates much of our social order. According to U.N. reports, nearly 10 million children die every year from starvation and preventable diseases such as dysentery.[50] That's more than 27,000 a day! And there are hundreds of millions more living with pain and suffering from some unnecessary, nonfatal, disease. That's indifference.

A small percentage of belligerent people who are indifferent to others are shaping the world for the rest of us. I saw a good example of this attitude while looking out the window one morning while eating breakfast. A small bird on the lawn in front of our house was eating a dandelion, a small weed that sprouts up out of the ground. There were lots of dandelions, perhaps thirty or forty. As the bird was tugging off pieces and swallowing them, suddenly another bird, the same type and size, swooped down and scared the bird away. Then the new bird started eating the same dandelion.

Since there were lots of dandelions, the first bird moved to another one. Suddenly, the second bird again flew at the first bird causing it to fly away again. Content with the abundance of dandelions, the first bird moved on to another—only once again to be chased away. The second, aggressive bird continued this behavior until it drove the first bird away from the dandelions altogether.

Those who oppose freedom from want are like that second bird. They hoard all the dandelions for themselves when there are more than enough to go around. Fortunately, humans are smart enough to be able to construct an enforceable agreement through reading and writing that does not allow brutes to take all of our resources, including our human resources, for themselves. We humans are no better than the birds without the rule of law. Indeed, we lived without it for centuries, and plenty of people still behave that way. But the times are changing. Today there is an emerging movement to make economic and social rights, such as education and health care, enforceable in courts of law.[51]

Let's be clear, however, about just how far we as an international community are willing to go to restrain the aggressive bird hogging all the dandelions.

To some extent it is good that the assertive bird is trying to take extra dandelions. It's okay, that there is this impulse. Besides, there is no denying it because it is part of the human condition. Humans, like other animals, have evolved by going around and taking whatever they can get. This impulse can be valuable when it leads to ingenuity, hard work, and the drive to get ahead.

The difficulty arises, however, with the excessively greedy bird. If you think back to what I saw that morning during breakfast, the second bird, the greedy bird, would not let the first bird have *any* dandelions. This is essentially where we are today with our local and international social systems. The greedy birds are taking much more than they need. Take food, for example. More than enough food is prepared each day in homes and restaurants to feed every human on earth adequately, yet millions are starving, as much of this food is wasted or thrown out.

The fact is there are enough dandelions to go around, even if some greedy birds hoard batches of them. We can, and should, have an imbalance in possession and consumption. Initiative and hard work should be rewarded; few poor people will disagree with this. Few people today claim that everything should be divided equally. I don't hear this claim in my classroom, and I haven't heard it in other classrooms either. Laziness is not to be rewarded with riches. Nevertheless, you will hear students and others say they want equality of opportunity. They want the tools to compete. They don't want the rich kids to be able to buy their way into a good education while the public schools flounder.

The idea of a right to a good public education is not new and it is a crucial component of freedom from want. Thomas Jefferson started the first American public university, the University of Virginia. He understood what was true then and now, that without a proper education it is difficult to compete in business and participate in a republic. Freedom from want ensures that everyone has a decent opportunity to succeed in business and politics; the rest is up to them.

Providing opportunity has both local and international ramifications. Locally, in the United States, only 25 percent of students go on to college and 2,500 teenagers drop out of high school every day.[52] While much of this is personal choice and lack of interest, it also results from the limited number of positions available in four-year universities. Competition is fierce, absurdly so. At the University of California, Berkeley, for example, in 2009 thousands of students with perfect 4.0 grade-point averages in high school were denied admission. And just think of the many thousands who had less than perfect grades when they were in high school, myself included. The result of these high grade requirements is that by the end of the ninth or tenth grade even exceptional students are being "weeded out." There is nothing wrong with meritocracy, but too few places in universities can lead to widespread disillusionment. Many students at a young age feel there is no place for them in college, so they give up, drop out, and end up involved in crime or making other choices at odds with society.[53]

There are similar examples in the international area. Through the Internet and other means entire peoples are becoming aware that they are being left behind; this leads to a perceived inequality that can create an atmosphere of conflict. The people of Afghanistan and Pakistan are among the poorest in the world. Of course, jealousy and resentment result. Jealousy, both conscious and subconscious, spreads throughout the world with the speed of a pandemic and then manifests itself in religious fundamentalism and other extremes that give people a sense of purpose and belonging when they feel left out from mainstream society. They don't start out on the fringe; they are relegated there.

Fortunately, just as there is enough food to go around, there is also enough money to go around. The triumph of capitalism as the global economic system creates a unique moment of opportunity. Capitalism as a system generates great wealth along with ingenuity and productivity, so much so that we can have stratification and still provide a decent life for all. We don't need to put large segments of society on the fringe. What is also clear, however, is that capitalism consolidates wealth. In the United States, and much of Europe and Latin America, the top 2 percent of the people now have over 70 percent of all wealth. The power of 2048 is that it creates and protects a middle class in all countries at a time when wealth is consolidating into the hands of fewer and fewer people. 2048 maximizes the potential of capitalism by ensuring that everyone has an opportunity to compete in the marketplace; 2048 helps bring about a peaceful resolution of social pressures, which if left unaddressed will eventually lead to violent revolution and police states.

Humanity's innate yearning for justice includes economic justice. Just as people will fight and die for free speech, they will fight and die for a redistribution of wealth if the imbalance becomes too great. If we reach the point, and we are not far from it, where 2 percent of the people on our spinning blue-and-green planet have 80 percent of all wealth, then history will be poised not for an agreement to live together, but for continual social upheaval, whether it is expressed in religious movements, class movements, or both. Regardless of good or bad economic times, or which political parties are in power, wealth is accumulating in fewer and fewer hands.[54] Presently 80 percent of humanity lives on less than $10 dollars a day.[55] Without the realization of freedom from want for everyone in the world these social pressures will erupt, and not everyone rebelling will be a "terrorist." It is not surprising that rebellion will erupt if the Five Freedoms continue to go unmet and unprotected by the rule of law. The preamble to the

Universal Declaration of Human Rights foretells exactly this possibility and attempts to avert it. The preamble states:

> Whereas it is essential, if man is not to be compelled to have recourse, as a last resort, to rebellion against tyranny and oppression, that human rights should be protected by the rule of law.

The charge is clear: human rights should be protected by the rule of law to avoid recourse to rebellion. What can be expected since there was no climate change agreement when the countries of the world met in Copenhagen, Denmark in December, 2009? Our younger generations are realizing they will be left on a planet with a ruined ecosystem because of greedy birds who want to maintain the status quo. At what point do they have the right to start destroying the things that are destroying the ecosystem? Should human rights continue to remain unenforceable, including environmental rights, we can expect there to be rebellion and upheaval.

The way to avoid rebellion is for the wealthiest among us to share a few dandelions. Not all, but some. As was explained by Raghavan Iyer, in his classic *Parapolitics:*

> The litmus test for the integrity and continuity of a social system is a confident or reluctant commitment of the privileged to denying themselves some opportunities for the sake of new entrants."[56]

Happily, there is a growing group of business and entertainment leaders who are willing to make room for new entrants. These leaders are humble enough to realize that the immense wealth they have accumulated is due to both their own hard work and to the society that enabled them. They recognize that the "self-made" man is rarely self-made.

Ted Turner, Bill Gates, and Warren Buffet, among others, recognize that society empowered them and they, in turn, are empowering society. They, like the publisher of this book, Berrett-Koehler, want to create "a world that works for all," and they have the drive to figure out how this can happen. 2048 enables them to achieve this goal. The freedom from want that is part of 2048 does not create a school here or a school there or a new hospital wing, it sets a social order in motion that provides them, as President Roosevelt said, "everywhere in the world."

If we are to have schools and hospitals everywhere, then it's logical to figure out how many we need, and how we would staff them. We use the term "humanistics" in 2048. It's a blend of two words, humanity and statistics. The term is used to debunk the myth that there is not enough to go around. Although you seldom hear the comment made outright because it is so callous, there is a concern lurking in most of us that there is not enough to go around and, therefore, each country, and in some instances each community, had better take what it can. Through the use of humanistics, we can think together about what it would take to truly have the full realization of human rights for all, without jumping to the assumption that there is not enough to go around.

Humanistics is a needs assessment not unlike what we do to decide when to build another road. If a new road is to be built, traffic engineers collect statistics to determine how many cars pass in certain directions and certain times. So too with rights, whether it is health care or free speech, it's worthwhile to think through what it will take to provide these rights for everyone in the world. Sometimes humanistics appear daunting, but only by thinking through needs on a global scale can we make a legitimate assessment of how they can be met. We've had enough platitudes about what everyone should have, and now it's time to figure out what it will really take to provide all rights for all people. Once we know clearly what we need to do, not only for our own local community or our national community, but also for our international community, we can initiate a blend of private and governmental entrepreneurship to meet these needs.

For example, if the optimum class size is twenty students per teacher for elementary school, then we need to divide by twenty the total number of elementary-school-age children in the world. The same formula can be applied for brain surgeons and every other group. Admittedly, this is not a fixed formula, and wide variations are surely inevitable, depending on unique circumstances. But the number of brain surgeons should not be determined solely by the number of people who can afford to pay for them. I am not suggesting that we can figure out a perfect number and then just meet that number. What I am suggesting is that we can use humanistics to see just how out of balance we are in both our thinking and our provision. The point is to figure out the needs of our entire human family and think through how we are going to meet these needs, not through state socialism, or communism, but through capitalism and markets combined with public services.

The revelation that the wealthy have succeeded because of the society from which they have arisen, and their desire to share similar opportunities, will be profoundly instrumental in the prevention of war in the twenty-first and twenty-second centuries. I believe this realization will usher in a prolonged period of peace and prosperity. Once we recognize that freedom from want is of equal status with freedom of speech and freedom of religion, then we can build a society in which there are those who are rich and those who are becoming rich, and all live richly with a decent life.

Technology offers new ways to capture this moment and fund freedom from want. The Internet provides the ability for us to collect our financial resources as well as record our thoughts. Not all of the funding for freedom from want must come from wealthy individuals and foundations. The election of Barack Obama shows us how it is possible to pool small financial contributions, as small as $20, with tremendous results. Millions of people in the United States made their own choice, and using an Internet website as a collection point made Obama's campaign a success with their contributions. In a similar manner, millions of people internationally can accomplish reaching an agreement to live together.

Through 2048 individuals and nonprofits can pool their resources to craft an agreement to live together that ensures the full realization of freedom from want. "It is a fine line between the impossible and the inevitable."[57] The general will of the people is the bridge from one to the other. This moment calls for a bold step, not a short one.

Of course, it was not only small contributors who funded President Obama's campaign. Large contributors and organizations funded the network that empowered the individual donors. Without the provision of catalytic funding it is nearly impossible to organize masses of people. The result was a democratic social movement throughout the United States. The trend afoot is that many leaders of prominent foundations realize that they are the catalyst, not the solution, and that they can use new technological tools to empower the social movements of the general public. This turning point for philanthropy can carry forward the turning point for humanity.

Fortunately, it is not only philanthropists who are turning their sights toward the achievement of freedom from want. Well-established human rights organizations such as Amnesty International are also beginning to champion economic and social rights along with civil and political freedoms. The mission of Amnesty, like many other international human rights organizations, is to further the goals of the Universal Declaration of Human Rights. For many years Amnesty has made great strides in the field of civil and political rights, and it is now providing valuable leadership by moving to enforce the social and economic rights to education and health care, core rights within freedom from want.

Some people say that freedom from want is impossible to achieve because it's too expensive, but that's only because they have not genuinely added up the costs of the existing flawed social order. Take health care in America, for example. Every time there is a serious automobile accident in which people are permanently injured, a lawsuit follows to determine how much money they will need for continuing medical care throughout their lives. Experts are paid a fortune to try to figure this out. Even more foolish than this whole speculative inquiry is that once an astronomical number is figured out, then the lawyers keep 40 percent of these future funds that have been awarded for medical costs!

If freedom from want is included in our written agreement to live together, then universal health-care would be required and all this needless litigation could be eliminated. There would never be an issue about future health-care costs because health care would be provided for every person, whether he or she is the president of the country or a delivery truck driver. Tens of billions of dollars could be taken out of the pockets of experts and attorneys and put into the payment of doctors, where it belongs—not to mention the savings for our clogged courtrooms and what it costs to staff them.

Attorneys' fees in accident cases are just one example. The truth is that the cost of the lack of freedom from want is much greater than opponents to rights to education and health care will admit. Internationally, the economic costs of a lack of education are immense. For one, lack of education is directly related to the rise in terrorism. Greg Mortenson's international best seller, *Three Cups of Tea,* is recent and strong proof of the correlation between a lack of freedom from want and terrorism. As he explains from his experience building schools in Pakistan and Afghanistan, "I've learned that terror doesn't happen because some group of people somewhere like Pakistan and Afghanistan simply decide to hate us. It happens because children aren't being offered a bright enough future that they have a reason to choose life over death."[58] President Roosevelt would understand this. So does 2048. 2048 takes *Three Cups of Tea* to scale. Mortenson's observations about Pakistan and Afghanistan apply to much of the world.

Another reason to provide education "everywhere in the world" is that well-documented studies show that there is a direct correlation between providing secondary and university education, particularly to women, and a decline of the birth rate. Stabilizing the world's population is one of the best ways to make sure that there is enough to go around, so it makes sense to pay for fundamental freedoms such as education and health care. Indifference, in addition to being immoral, will also cost us more financially in the long run, in both lives and money, as the overpopulated world will be forced to fight over scarce resources. Another three billion people will join the 6.6 billion on this planet within the next fifty years. Today over 1.4 million people pour into the world's slums every week. The year 2048 is a little less than forty years away. We have a clear choice. Given the link between better education and a decline in fertility rates, through 2048 and the realization of freedom from want, by the 100th anniversary of the Universal Declaration we can drastically reduce current population trends. 2048 makes it possible to stabilize the world's population with people living with varying degrees of wealth, but all with decent lives.

The final and greatest cost from a lack of freedom from want is disease and death. As President Obama wrote in *The Audacity of Hope,* "It's in the misery of some unnamed slum that the next killer virus will emerge."[59] The ongoing pandemic of the swine flu is a poignant example. It began with a child living in poverty near a wretched pig farm in Mexico. Now it is worldwide. The only reason that tens of millions of people have not died is that the virus has proven to be less lethal than was first thought. As this book goes to press over one billion people have suffered through the swine flu! This is the direct result of a poor child living in wretched conditions and pigs living nearby in equally wretched conditions. How much longer will we let this go on? A near miss is another good reason for achieving freedom from want. If you, your child, or someone you know suffered through the fever, chills, and aches of the swine flu, then pass this book along—something has to be done.

CHAPTER 7

Freedom for the Environment

Al Gore has explained that "it is important to change light bulbs, but it's more important to change the law"

Freedom for the environment is life, not just our own lives, but the life of the planet Earth. As human rights are intertwined and interdependent, so too our lives are intertwined and interdependent with our environment. As former Vice President Al Gore has said, "The relationship we have to the natural world is not a relationship between 'us' and 'it'. It is us and we are of it."[60] Given that *three new species become extinct every hour,*[61] largely from global warming and other environmental degradation caused by humans, it is necessary to think of fundamental rights in a more holistic way. It's time for a fifth freedom: freedom for the environment.

Preservation of the Environment

The core of freedom for the environment is the preservation of what we have. By including the environment in our list of rights, it is possible to protect the environment when it is being despoiled and wildlife is being decimated. It means a better chance for science, rather than politics, to guide the outcome of major decisions impacting the environment. This is a huge accomplishment with a direct impact on people and other living creatures.

I grew up in the San Francisco Bay Area and enjoyed going salmon fishing with my father. It was a big event for us. We got up early and went out with the commercial boats. While some days were better than others, we almost always went home with fish at the end of the day. My father had also gone fishing with his father, and to continue the tradition and the fun I also took my sons salmon fishing when they were young. But not anymore. For two years now salmon fishing has been closed because the number of fish has been depleted to the point that the fish may not be able to recover. This story is not just an isolated incident in San Francisco. It's a common story all around the world.

Coincidental with the title of this book, a major report about our oceans was released with the title "Seafood May Be Gone by 2048."[62] According to this report in the journal *Science,* "Unless humans act now, seafood may disappear by 2048." The ocean has already lost 29 percent of its biodiversity, and, "if this trend continues in thirty years there will be little or no seafood available for sustainable harvest." This is exactly what has happened with the salmon in San Francisco: there are too few salmon available for sustainable harvest.

Even worse is that I saw this trend evolve right before my own eyes. I was counsel on cases in which I was trying to protect the few remaining old growth redwood trees next to rivers in northern California. The owner was clear-cutting trees, even next to the rivers. Without the shade canopy the trees provided, the water temperatures would rise and the young salmon would die. Unfortunately, the law was not strong enough to protect the salmon and the cases were lost. Now we are unable to fish for salmon because of excessive greed and a lack of law. These experiences show that law does matter. Our current agreement to live together was not strong enough to prevent the depletion of salmon until now when we cannot fish for them.

But the reason we must have freedom for the environment goes even further than these firsthand stories of environmental ruin. We are now experiencing environmental calamity on a global level. The rate of extinction of species on Earth is higher than at any point since the extinction of the dinosaurs. For those foolish enough to say that at least species came back after the demise of the dinosaurs, what they leave out is that the replenishment of species takes millions of years![65] There simply is not time to undo the havoc we are wreaking on this Earth—we must stop it. The first step is to take responsibility for the three species that become extinct each hour and commit ourselves to a plan like 2048 that will create enforceable law to stop this madness.

Our inclusion of the environment is not only for moral reasons, though these are sufficient; it's about the quality of life. Think for a moment about the finest moments in your life: what comes to mind? You probably think of relationships, mostly, the finest times with family, friends, and lovers. But what else? For many it's moments in the natural environment—hiking in the mountains, swimming in the seas, boating on rivers and lakes, running, biking, and even simply viewing sunrises and sunsets. Often the best moments in our relationships coincide with great moments in the environment.

When we connect with the environment we connect with ourselves. The wake of the surfboard or sailboat, or the tracks of skis or snowshoes, leave nothing on the Earth, but within us they leave lasting memories of exhilaration and satisfaction. They leave joy. It makes sense that we want to preserve these moments for ourselves and our children. It's better to take our children to the snows of Kilimanjaro than to tell them you can remember the snows of Kilimanjaro and it is something they never have a chance to experience.[64]

The change in times requires a change in freedoms. At the time that President Roosevelt stated the first Four Freedoms, we lacked an awareness of the rate at which resources were dwindling. Now we know that we are running out of water, forests, and fish, and that the prevalent view in the past that we are each free to take what we can from the environment will no longer work. With forests, for example, according to the United Nation's Environmental Programme, "Worldwide deforestation continues at an alarming rate, about 13 million hectares per year, an area the size of Greece or Nicaragua."[65]

The difficulty, however, is that while the vast majority of humanity recognizes the need for regulation of activities on our planet to protect our environment, "competition" among nations leads to a race to the bottom. Few are willing to restrain themselves voluntarily with environmental protections when others with no scruples seize the opportunity to take even more for themselves.

Establishing a new baseline of human rights law that includes the environment will put an end to this race to the bottom where we will all lose.[66] The problem of climate change has shown us that global problems require global solutions. The work of the environmental scientists from around the world who won the Nobel Peace Prize for their studies on global warming in 2008 shows it is possible to have a global collaborative effort to figure out global solutions. It makes sense to listen to experts, particularly when they can show that it will cost us more to do nothing about global warming now and later have to clean up after the consequences.[67] What is needed is a similar global collaborative effort to change the law to implement solutions, and 2048 facilitates that collaboration. By creating a fifth freedom, freedom for the environment, as part of an International Convention, we are changing the law, our agreement to live together, to adapt to the times.

Right to Participate in Decisions Affecting the Environment

Recognition of the right to freedom for the environment also advances our freedom of speech. For the most part, freedom of speech gives us the right to comment about what is occurring in government, but not necessarily the right to participate in policy decisions. Environmental rights, however, typically include the right of public participation in the decision-making process regarding projects that can have a substantial effect on the environment. At the very least, environmental rights ensure the opportunity to appear and to put important scientific information into the record so that policymakers must be transparent in their decisions and cannot ignore science. This aspect of freedom for the environment is essential. Even though the public today has relinquished the power to govern to those in government, it makes sense that for momentous decisions that impact people's daily lives and well-being the public should retain the opportunity to contribute to the decision-making process.

Protection for Future Generations

Finally, some things in life are given with the understanding that we will use them, enjoy them, and then pass them along so others may do the same. Intergenerational equity is another reason for freedom for the environment. Our children have a right to that which we enjoy.

At the very least, they are entitled to oceans with fish, air that's fit to breathe, food and water that are safe to eat and drink—the basic necessities of life. These have been in abundance throughout most of the existence of humanity. It is only in recent decades that we have so befouled the environment that resources are drastically depleted past the point of recovery unless there is an intervention. As parents and grandparents we have an obligation to assert ourselves and exercise a sufficient amount of our own personal power and assets to protect our children and their heritage. Marching and begging will not be enough. Those profiting from the decimation of the environment regardless of the impact on future generations have the money and political power to maintain the present disastrous course.

I will never forget when my 13-year-old son learned about global warming in school. He came home and asked me, not in a demanding, but in a searching, way: "How could your generation let this happen?" Honestly, I didn't have an answer. It's not that we don't know better. It's not that we don't have the means to switch to alternative energy. The answer that I didn't have then, but which is clear to me now, is that we are letting others run things when we should be accepting more responsibility for running them ourselves. For ourselves, and for our children, their children, and all species on this beautiful planet, it's time for us to provide freedom for the environment.

CHAPTER 8

Freedom from Fear

Mikhail Gorbachev, the father of Peristroika/Restructuring, helped bring about a transformation from the Cold War to an international community

Freedom from fear is our collective reward for the realization of the other Four Freedoms. It is a state of well-being. It is the confidence of knowing that we can speak freely about our government, and report corruption without fear of being taken to prison or losing our job. It is the comfort of a voluntary connection with God, or the right to choose no connection at all. It is the fulfillment of knowing that our children will be able to attend excellent schools from preschool up through completion of university and possibly graduate school. And it is the assurance that if any of us should fall ill from birth to death there will be health care equal to that available to the political officials who lead us. In short, freedom from fear is an everyday sense of well-being, whoever we are or wherever we might live.

Freedom from fear also reflects the well-being we feel from being part of an interconnected international community instead of only a group of quarrelsome nation-states spending trillions of dollars and constantly preparing to annihilate one another. There is a daily psychic toll from hearing that war is imminent or that another pandemic is making its way out of wretched poverty and into all our homes. We can rid ourselves from these constant anxieties. The emergence of tolerance and cooperation in Europe following two major world wars shows tangibly how freedom from fear can be achieved.

Rule of Law

Another aspect of freedom from fear is the creation of an independent judiciary everywhere in the world. It is not enough to put rights on paper, they must be enforceable. A Bill of Rights without enforcement is a fairy tale. Enforcement requires an independent evaluator. It's impossible to write words in such a manner that there will not be disagreement about them. Human beings will always have disputes and some of these disputes will be about the meaning of the words within an International Convention on Human Rights. The U.S. Bill of Rights and the French Declaration of the Rights of Man, the two oldest written Bills of Rights (which were prepared at approximately the same time), are over 200 years old, yet cases continue to arise regarding their interpretation, and they always will. Just as our social contract continually evolves, the documents that embody that contract also continue to evolve.

Why are judges and not politicians charged with protection and enforcement of our written social contract? First, there is an expectation that politicians will indeed protect and enforce our agreement to live together. Part of that agreement is that representatives will support the rights listed in our agreement in exchange for the power we give them to govern. This is why we require politicians to take an oath swearing to uphold the law embodied in our bills of rights. We also recognize, however, that there are many influences on politicians and that inherently "power corrupts." So in addition to this pledge, we create a body of independent neutral judges to ensure that politicians will keep their word.[68]

It's not that judges have a perfect understanding of the wording in an International Convention on Human Rights, or any other Bill of Rights, but rather because they have a specific role of neutrality and impartiality. Some may be skeptical that such neutrality can be maintained, but we have seen for thousands of years, throughout history and across cultures, how the evolution of society has been inextricably intertwined with the selection of neutral decision makers among us, whether among indigenous tribes or in metropolitan areas. One of our great character traits as human beings is the ability to resolve disputes among ourselves fairly and impartially, based on presentation of disputes to neutral parties. Freedom from fear and 2048 rest solidly on this ability. This is one of our finest qualities as humans.

Let me provide three role models for these claims about judicial character. The first is the Hon. Thelton Henderson, a U.S. District Court judge, who is African-American. The next is the late Hon. Harold Fong, a U.S. District Court judge, who is Asian-American. The third is the Hon. Jon Tigar, a California Superior Court judge, who is Caucasian. Judge Fong and Judge Tigar were appointed by Republicans; Judge Henderson was appointed by a Democrat.

The reason I mention the ethnicity and political backgrounds of all three is that I want to show the autonomy of judicial character. I knew Judge Fong and I continue to see and talk with Judge Henderson and Judge Tigar. Despite their racial and political differences, I can say confidently that when they put on their black robes they put their dedication to the U.S. Constitution before their personal backgrounds and interests. Of course, no judge can ever fully remove the influence of his or her own background on his or her opinions; however, the neutrality of the same black robe that they wear reflects the dedication to the rule of law that they all share.

While the ability to judge impartially is one of humanity's greatest traits, judges may also succumb to the influence of power. Power can corrupt judges as well as politicians. Therefore, there should be checks and balances for judges, just as there are for elected officials. To this end, it is important that there are layers of review for judges. Security comes from knowing that any of us can walk into the local court and the same set of fundamental human rights will be enforced. One of the great achievements of 2048 is that it creates a set of rights in a single document that can be enforced in the courts of all countries. That said, because decision makers' political and personal biases can alter their ability to resolve disputes fairly, there should be a framework in which higher bodies review local decisions in order to thwart corruption and reinforce the rule of law.

Regardless of the level of judicial review, whether it's a local court, a state supreme court, a transnational court such as the European Court of Human Rights, or an International Court of Human Rights, judges are required to think beyond their own intellectual and professional backgrounds and strive to articulate a decision that can easily be understood by all people.

Society flourishes with the rule of law. The rule of law also creates freedom from fear by establishing a process, a system of law, so that no person, or nation, with the biggest club can bully the others. Law, not whim or heredity, governs. Kings and queens may exist, but their power is given to them by the people, and there is no reason to fear them. And when any of our rights are violated, no matter where we are traveling, or where we are from, whether we are engaged in business or pleasure, there should be the security of knowing that there is something we can do about any violation of our rights. With 2048 in place we can go to court in any country and stand before an impartial person, or perhaps a group of people such as a jury, and ask that our social contract embodied in law be enforced. Then orders by the court can be issued against anyone who violates our agreement to live together so that it is always more than just a piece of paper.

Of course, there are pros and cons to having matters resolved through courts,[69] but through the rule of law our freedoms are more than mere statements or aspirations. They are binding and enforceable by judges who are committed to the law, allowing us all to live in freedom from fear, with all Five Freedoms in place.

Disarmament

Disarmament is also a part of freedom from fear and is linked with freedom from want. It is a legitimate concern that countries will continue to spend unwisely on their militaries even as international funds are being channeled into them for schools and hospi-

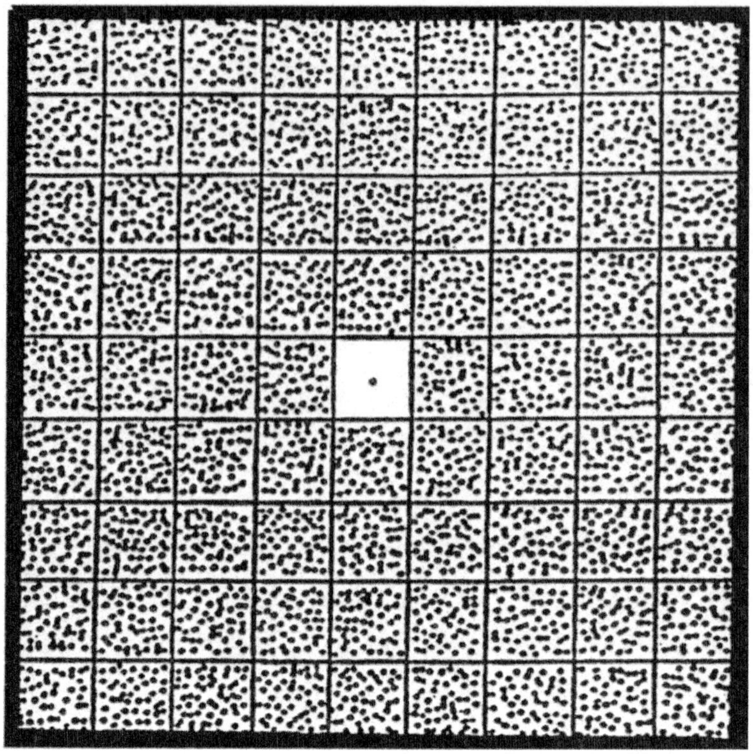

tals. Countries that receive funds as part of the alleviation of freedom from want should not be permitted to redirect expenditures to bombs from funds intended for their schools and hospitals. Given that one of the primary purposes of 2048 is a new form of international security based on collective respect for rights rather than reliance on the military, the distribution of funds to overcome freedom from want should be conditioned on demilitarization.

But demilitarization should not be applied only to poorer countries. Affluent countries have as much, or more, to gain from demilitarization as part of the realization of freedom from fear. Roosevelt made it very clear that the overarching goal of demilitarization is to reduce military might to the point where no country is a military threat to any other. In giving his explanation he stated:

> Translated into world terms, freedom from fear means worldwide reduction of armaments to such a point and in such a thorough fashion that no nation will be in a position to commit an act of physical aggression against any neighbor—everywhere in the world.

Despite Roosevelt's wonderful leadership, our international community has gone in the opposite direction from disarmament, and instead has stockpiled massive amounts of arms, including thousands of nuclear weapons on hair-trigger status at all times. Such stockpiles are a waste of our human and financial resources. A look at the diagram above demonstrates this point.

If you look at the dot in the center of the picture, it represents the total amount of explosive power, bombs, and other weapons used in World War II. This includes the firebombing of Dresden, the nightly bombing of London, and the atomic bombs dropped on Hiroshima and Nagasaki. Now look at the hundreds of dots around that one in the center. They represent the ever-increasing amount of explosive power, including nuclear bombs and other weapons, which fill our arsenals today!

Freedom from fear will be impossible to achieve as long as there continues to be a flood of weapons into our international community. The United States sells more military weapons than any other country.[70] Often the weapons used to kill American soldiers were made in America. One frequently hears pundits rage against the "bureaucracy" of the United Nations, but the Pentagon is the second largest building in the world (after Beijing airport). The Central Intelligence Agency has more employees than the United Nations.[71] This is wasteful. All countries can still continue to have military preparedness, but some of the resources need to be redirected to achieve security in other ways. We need to make many of the dots in the diagram represent schools, hospitals, and courthouses, instead of bombs.

Our disarmament should not only involve conventional weapons, but nuclear weapons as well. Why do we continue to have large stockpiles of nuclear weapons? Against whom can we possibly use them all? Does the United States need nuclear weapons to protect itself from Canada? From Mexico? Is it really likely that any country will actually try to attack and take American soil? European soil? Russian soil? Chinese soil? It's not. Why? Not because the United States, Europe, Russia, and China have nuclear weapons, but because people will fight to the death for their countries. Borders exist not only because they deter military action, but because of established norms, including the right of states to maintain their own boundaries. Documents and courtrooms are a more effective, less costly, and safer deterrent than nuclear weapons.

So that leaves terrorism. Is it conceivable that we would ever use a nuclear weapon against terrorists? No. Why? Because if we ever need to use a nuclear weapon against terrorists, then they are already more than just terrorists, they are a political movement. Nuclear weapons cause such widespread death and destruction that the only rationale for using them would be against large numbers of people. We will have failed as an international community if there is such a widespread following for a terrorist group that we would consider the need for a nuclear weapon. Terrorism may be organized by a few wealthy megalomaniacs, but it can rise as a movement only amidst large pockets of poverty, injustice, and discontent. As President Roosevelt said, "Freedom from fear is eternally linked with freedom from want."[72] Wiping out poverty will do more to rid the world of terrorism than any number of nuclear weapons will ever do. Terrorism will fade away as the Five Freedoms take hold. By strengthening and harmonizing the regional agreements to live together, which we will consider in the next chapter, we can live in freedom from fear by the year 2048.

PART THREE

WHERE THE 2048 MOVEMENT IS HEADED

CHAPTER 9

Regional Agreements to Live Together

The good news is that major portions of humanity's agreement to live together have already been written! There are several transnational regional human rights documents such as the European Convention on Human Rights, the African Convention on Human Rights, and the American Convention on Human Rights that have already taken the "first steps" toward humanity's written agreement to live together. These regional documents cover 60 percent of all people in the world. It is now time to reach the other 40 percent and tie all of these regions together through an International Convention on Human Rights with an International Court of Human Rights to enforce it. Through regional courts and an international court, all interpreting the same International Bill of Rights, we will finally make our fundamental rights enforceable for all of our human family—not just for a chosen few.

René Cassin led the "first steps" from the Universal Declaration of Human Rights to the European Convention on Human Rights

European Court of Human Rights

2048 is not just an inspirational goal or wishful thinking. We can see how a well-written list of rights, with courts to enforce it, is working today in Europe. While there are other regional courts, the European Court is discussed here because it is the most developed. After centuries of fighting, Europeans have agreed on the European Convention on Human Rights, a transnational document that applies in the courts of 47 countries and is enforced by the European Court of Human Rights, which has judges from all 47 countries. As René Cassin, one of the founders of the European Court and one of its first judges, said when he won the Nobel Peace Prize for his work drafting the European Convention, "It works."

And the European Convention works on the paths of everyday life as well as in courtrooms. Today there is a bridge near the city of Strasbourg, France, the home of the European Court of Human Rights. On one side of the bridge a visitor is in France, on the other, Germany. There is no border checkpoint. You can walk across. But to take those steps, first millions of people had to give their lives to defeat fascism and tyranny. Next, millions more had to take the mental step of breaking their chains by choosing to create a new social order based on the rule of law instead of the rule of force. 2048 is an international movement to follow these courageous souls and take further steps to build similar bridges among all nations.

One of the main reasons for the European court's success is the requirement that any state that wishes to be part of the Council of Europe, a political and trade organization with many economic benefits, must agree to have the European Convention of Human Rights as part of its domestic law and enforceable in its domestic courts. This connection between entry into the European trade club and acceptance of a binding human rights document is an important lesson for the rest of the world.

Now that capitalism has prevailed as the predominant international economic order, and all countries, along with their multinational corporations, want to engage in international markets, it is possible for us to follow the European example and to require that in order for a country to participate in the World Trade Organization it must agree to accept an International Convention on Human Rights as enforceable within its domestic law. This parallel approach to what has worked so well in Europe is one of the best ways to achieve in a simple and even-handed way the enforcement of an International Bill of Human Rights in all countries.

It is also important that the judges of the European Court do not sit only to represent the interests of their home countries; rather, all must serve the European Convention they are interpreting and must be true to the social contract that is the essence of the European Convention. Even if they do not personally agree with a portion of the Convention, they must follow the wording of the document. In addition, judges must be willing to hold the leaders from their own countries accountable if those leaders act in violation of the Convention. In sum, each judge must put the wording and the spirit of the European Convention above all else—above even a personal or national interest.

Of course, when there are regional or international agreements there are always issues of federalism, that is, the concern that the individual countries will be diminished by the concentration of power in a regional institution such as the European Court of Human Rights. But the European experience has shown that there is more to be gained than lost through a transnational agreement to live together that is enforceable in a regional court of law. One of the primary reasons that the European governments joined together in the European Convention is to prevent war, and they have succeeded. True, there are times when the highest court decisions of some countries, even the House of Lords of Great Britain, have been overturned by the European Court of Human Rights, but these instances have been few and far between, and for the most part what Europeans have found is that they share common values about fundamental rights.

I will not go into many cases here, but the case of *McDonald's Corporation v. Steel and Morris* is a good example.[73] The two plaintiffs, David Morris and Helen Steel, distributed pamphlets alleging that the McDonald's Corporation exploited child labor, caused serious damage to the rainforest, stifled union membership, and provided unsafe working conditions. McDonald's sued them claiming it had been defamed. The British High Court ordered Morris and Steel to pay damages to McDonald's for defamation. Morris and Steel appealed to the European Court of Human Rights. The European Court reversed the British High Court and ordered that damages be paid to Morris and Steel.[74] "The McDonald's case is not the only example of the success of the European court. While the dynamic between individual states and the European Court is not in perfect harmony, recent literature shows an impressive record of success.[75] Most important, every decision by the European Court of Human Rights has been followed by the domestic courts of the country in which the case arose! This demonstrates how a transnational court can succeed. The European Court decisions have been followed, not because of guns (because the European Court does not have any guns), but out of respect for the rule of law.

Of course, there will always be power issues between individual states and transnational courts, just as there are always power issues between individual states in the United States and the U.S. government. This tension is a strength, not a detriment. The interplay between the individual state supreme courts and the U.S. Supreme Court is an intricate dance that works well. For the most part the U.S. Supreme Court stays away from cases in which the state supreme court can make its own decisions based on its own constitution, and the European Court of Human Rights has done the same. Those who fear tyranny from a transnational court do not have the facts to justify their fears.

The composition of the courts is an important way to alleviate some of the concerns about power consolidating at the transnational level. The European Court of Human Rights includes judges from all 47 countries that are parties to the Convention, and every panel of judges hearing a case includes a judge from the country in which the case arose. This is not so that the native judges will have a bias in favor of their own countries, but rather so that they can share their familiarity with their countries' system with the other judges. However, in the end, all the judges, including the judge from the country where the case arose, remain committed to the European Convention and not to their national judiciary or national politicians.

The European Court of Human Rights has also shown through its decisions that it will go out of its way to give discretion and flexibility to the supreme courts of the various states. The European Court has developed what is called a "margin of appreciation." The margin of appreciation applies in cases arising from individual countries to the European Court. It provides for some flexibility so that some countries, based on their cultural differences, may have different outcomes, even when the court is interpreting the exact same language in the European Convention.[76]

Given the leeway that the European Court gives to the state supreme courts in their decisions, it is evident that the state courts are not being trampled on. The result is that Europe has gained more than it has lost by ending centuries of war while maintaining flexibility and respect for the laws of individual states. This same spirit of cooperation also resides within the preparation of documents, as was evident during the drafting of the Universal Declaration, the

European Convention and the Rome Statute for the International Criminal Court. Now there is a similar spirit for writing an International Convention on Human Rights. This is how social movements develop, with a sense of purpose combined with cooperation. The two together make the difference between having a fleeting effect and a long-term one. The European Convention provides the best protection for human rights in the world today, and it is a good model for other regional courts and an International Convention on Human Rights, to which we now turn.

CHAPTER 10

Humanity's Agreement to Live Together

Eleanor Roosevelt with the beginning of humanity's written agreement to live together

Now that we've looked back to see the evolution and predecessors of humanity's agreement to live together, and seen how regional agreements—particularly the European Convention on Human Rights, are developing—we are ready to look forward and think about an agreement to live together that includes our entire international community. This is what lies at the end of the turning point: an International Convention on Human Rights. Ralph

Waldo Emerson said, "Greatness appeals to the future," and through our document we make our appeal.[77]

There are many different opinions about what should be the framework for enforceable human rights in all countries. I value this marketplace of ideas so much that I am spending a major portion of my life collecting views that differ from my own. But here is my view: The time has come to take all the various documents that have been created, including the U.N. conventions and the regional conventions, and consolidate them into a single document that can be enforceable in the courts of all countries. So far I have not heard of or read of a better plan, but I intend to keep listening and reading.

Incrementalism has been useful to bring us to this point where we can now consolidate all existing documents into a single document, but incrementalism will no longer suffice. With global warming having progressed to the point where we may have irreparably damaged our planet, and with 27,000 men, women, and children dying each day needlessly from malnutrition and easily treatable illness, we've had enough incrementalism.[78] It's time to finish the turn, not crawl along on the periphery of the road.

I also want to be clear, however, that I'm not suggesting that we discard what we have. Rather, I am suggesting that we build on what exists. For example, even though the decisions of the Human Rights Committee, the committee responsible for enforcing the Covenant on Civil and Political Rights, are not enforceable, the *thinking* in those decisions is invaluable for the 2048 dialogue about an enforceable agreement to live together. These decisions provide a good starting point for discussing a broad range of rights and fortunately they are being compiled in books for easy reference.[79]

As valuable as the Human Rights Committee decisions are, however, human rights will never be fully realized as long as people subjected to the violation of their rights have to wait for a response from Geneva. Reporting to Geneva will never be enough in a world where there are frequent violations of rights. The U.N. system should be strengthened while preparations are being made to put an international convention into effect, but it is wise that the European Court of Human Rights lies outside and independent of the United Nations, and the International Court of Human Rights created by the International Convention on Human Rights should also lie outside and independent of the United Nations.

This chapter is linked with the last five chapters of this book, which lay out a process for the creation of a single document that can be enforceable in the courts of all countries. The most up-to-date full text of the draft International Convention can always be found on the 2048 website. The beauty of the draft International Convention is that it is something tangible that together we can focus on, think about, rewrite, and, finally, decide to implement in the courts of all countries.

Cultural Myths

Just as we have dispelled the myths that we must always live with war and that there are not enough resources to go around, let us now dispel some additional myths, beginning with the idea that creating an International Convention is a violation of culture.[80] Some claim that the creation of genuinely enforceable human rights for all people "everywhere in the world" is cultural imperialism. They disregard that the rights in the Universal Declaration of Human Rights are "universal." Fundamental human rights are derived from the existence of the human being. It doesn't matter whether those human beings are Chinese, British, or Nigerian—only that they live, that they exist. Every person is human; therefore, every person has human rights, including the Five Freedoms.

Those who wish to stymie the realization of human rights in accordance with the Universal Declaration are pleased with academic conversation and confrontation over whether fundamental rights such as free speech are truly universal. As long as we are in an endless cycle of conversation and controversy about this, we will not get to the *enforcement* of basic human rights. It is appropriate for there to be criticism of the rights set forth in the draft International Convention based on arguments of cultural relativism, but no one should disagree that there is a core set of fundamental rights that everyone is entitled to—such as freedom from slavery.

Typically, the denial of the universality of rights is actually an attempt to maintain the status quo and thwart the naturally expanding nature of rights. In many instances the people of our international community are prepared to expand their core set of rights to accept equality for women and health care for all even if their government leaders do not want to recognize these rights. The real violation of culture is to prevent this natural evolution of rights. For example, many of the one million girls each year who are pressured to have their clitoris removed as part of the cultural practice of female genital mutilation are now questioning the procedure as a violation of their rights. And they should, regardless of the cultural history of this ritual. The world has a long cultural history of slavery, but thankfully we did not allow that to freeze in place based on a misguided claim of cultural practice.

To the extent that there are countries that do not recognize the fundamental rights set forth in the Universal Declaration even though they have signed the document, there is reason to challenge them, not to roll over and accept their claims on the basis of "cultural differences." That they may be culturally resistant is not an argument for doing nothing in the name of cultural sanctity. To the contrary, the failure to bring about full realization of rights embodied in the Universal Declaration, is a reason *for* an enforceable document such as an International Convention, not a reason against such a document.

Human rights are innate yearnings in human beings that manifest themselves through a social contract, which is embodied in documents and, eventually, enforceable through the rule of law. Free speech is a good example. The people of China have an innate yearning, as all people do, to speak their minds. Take, for example, the Chinese man who took photographs depicting the poor construction of schools that had collapsed in the 2009 earthquake. His reward: He was convicted and given hard labor for exercising his innate right to free speech. Is there a cultural excuse for this? No.

Some might respond with equal vigor, Yes! Let them do so. And they may point to many Chinese citizens who will say they are willing to give up free speech for the sake of social stability. Surely slaves were conditioned to believe they were slaves and always would be, so they should just accept it and many did. Similarly, there are surely girls who want to have their clitoris removed when they are 10 years old because they have been indoctrinated to believe it is something that they must do. The simple truth is that the innate yearnings of human beings most often manifest themselves first among a minority, but they are *unstoppable.* Just as surely as there will be health care in the United States, there will one day be free speech in Iran, Russia, and elsewhere.

It is also parochial to assume that people leaving traditional villages for a modern life, including education, is a bad thing. To be sure, there are legitimate concerns about the departure of youth from stable societies, but in many families academic success is considered to be a virtue. Eleanor Roosevelt wrote about a picture taken of a father and son in the Philippines.[81] The father was a headhunter from the bush and in either hand he held a skull. The son beside him wore a white suit and glasses and carried a small professional bag. He was a trained physician, working in the field of public health. It's wrong to make either a good or a bad judgment about this picture. What matters most is how *they* felt about the picture and about each other.

Another problem is that cultural claims often do not reflect the current state of affairs. Again, take health care in the United States. There is no legal right to health care in America, and there never has been, despite the fact that the United States signed the Universal Declaration of Human Rights and polls show *that the majority of Americans believe that there is a right to health care.* I know a woman who was diagnosed with uterine tumors the size of baseballs. She could not receive emergency attention because the condition was not immediately life threatening, and she could not purchase health insurance, even though she was willing to pay, because her condition was "preexisting;" no company would cover her treatment costs. This was a gross violation of her human rights.

When asked during a presidential debate whether health care is a "right" or a "responsibility," then candidate Barack Obama said "it is a right." So what is correct? Even though most Americans agree with the president that health care is a right, those trying to maintain the status quo claim American culture does not recognize health care as a human right. Often, as is the case in America with health care, the claims of cultural relativism are already outdated when they are made. Cultural relativism is used as a pawn to stop the natural evolution of new cultural norms.

Even though I am suggesting that claims of cultural relativism should be viewed carefully, this is not to say that there should be no variation in the interpretation of the rights described within a document like an International Convention on Human Rights. The main problem with cultural relativism is that some people argue that it is improper to think of a list of rights at all because they assume no list will work for all countries. This is wrong. Cultural relativism does not justify stopping the development of universal human rights. It is better if cultural variations are taken into consideration when court decisions are written about the applications of rights, rather than not have any list at all.

Finally, anyone who makes the accusation that the International Convention is a Western document is mistaken. Many Eastern societies have put a greater emphasis on freedom from want than have countries in the West. Similarly, those who assume that fidelity to the rule of law is only a Western conception are also mistaken.[82] One of the accomplishments of 2048 will be that the East will accept freedom of speech and freedom of religion while the West will accept freedom from want. There is no cultural imperialism, rather there is a merging of universal human rights into the social contract for all people.

Sovereignty Myths

As we prepare to draft an International Convention, let's also dispel the myth that nations will never agree to an International Convention because they will lose their "sovereignty." First, who is the "sovereign"? It is the people, not the government. The only sovereignty that governments have is what the people have voluntarily given them. All power emanates from the people; therefore, the government is not giving up anything if the people decide that they wish to revise their social contract.

If, as is the case with the European Convention, the people of all countries decide that they want to have a transnational court to resolve their disputes rather than pay $1.4 trillion toward military expenditures each year and live in the shadow of war and nuclear annihilation, it's their choice, and it is a wise one. Governments cannot deny the people their right to reach an enforceable agreement to live together. Kings may behave this way, but not republics.

A good recent example is the Charter of Fundamental Rights for the European Union. This charter passed its last hurdle in November 2009, and will now become an enforceable bill of rights. The Charter includes *education, health care, and environmental* rights! If you set the European Charter next to the draft International Convention you will see that they are similar. We are getting closer to our agreement to live together, and we can make it by the year 2048.

Given how close we are, it's time for the people in all nations to assert themselves and make rights enforceable. 2048 as a movement places an emphasis on self-reliance to complete our agreement. It was impressive that President Obama included Emerson's essay on "Self-Reliance" when he published his inaugural address.[83] Obama cast aside societal assumptions about what could and could not be done, and was elected despite the odds against him. So too we should follow the advice of Emerson and cast aside invalid claims of sovereignty by governments, and exercise our own sovereignty. Emerson said:

> Let us affront and reprimand the smooth mediocrity and squalid contentment of the times, and hurl in the face of custom and trade and office.

Humanity wants to fulfill its destiny to become a human family. Two hundred years from now, our international differences will be no greater than the differences today among the nations of Europe. The Enlightenment is not over; it continues. The idea of enforceable rights has come a long way and is spreading throughout Europe, the Middle East, Africa, and Asia as well. The European Convention and other regional documents have shown us that a melting pot of nations, with enforceable fundamental rights for all, is possible. The International Convention, like the European, African, and American Conventions today, will be the core law of the land. "Law" is simply our agreement to live together, and the International Convention will constitute humanity's agreement to live together.

Now that we have cleared away all the myths restricting the exercise of our free will to draft and implement an International Convention, in the following chapters we turn to the next steps we can all take on our path to create a single document that can be enforceable in all countries.

CHAPTER 11

The Path Together

Charles Malik, from Lebanon, guided the Universal Declaration through the United Nations process for the benefit of these children and future generations

Now it's time to draft humanity's agreement to live together so that by the year 2048 we will have enforceable human rights for all people. The following four chapters, and the ongoing 2048 Project at the Berkeley Law School, separate the 2048 plan from statements of aspiration. Considering what has been done by others, these chapters explain how to move forward: First we *focus together;* this is mustering the will to act. Then we *think together;* we put our minds in parallel position by thinking together about what is optimum. Next we *write together;* we capture our thoughts by writing them down. Finally, we *decide together* which writing we want to keep and which to discard. We began with Five Freedoms and we end with four steps to make them part of our daily lives. The result is humanity's written agreement to live together.

The four steps are not difficult, but they do take an act of faith. Here I'm not talking about religious faith—I'm talking about faith in ourselves. I widely circulated this manuscript before this book went to print. Some were skeptical that the "common people" will care enough to join a movement like 2048. This skepticism underestimates the depth of understanding and concern people throughout the world have for human rights. One of my favorite reviewers is the parking lot attendant at the building where the 2048 Project is located. A broad base of people is willing to participate, and even glad that they are being asked. As long as we have been discarding myths along the way, let's also discard the myth that only lawyers or people with some professional expertise can write our agreement to live together. Humanity today does not look only within legal and political ranks for leadership, and properly so.

One place this leadership can be found is in the arts. Many in the arts (and I broadly include actors, talk show hosts, and musicians, along with painters, writers, and sculptors) are our trendsetters. They are leaders ahead of our political representatives when it comes to social movements, and they can be the catalyst for 2048. The arts often transcend our national, religious, racial, and other differences, and prepare us to question whether these differences are really the seeds of conflict or the seeds of creativity and love. Beauty is the guide for art, and it is beauty that guides us down the 2048 path together. Our task is to focus, think, write, and decide together to create the most beautiful Bill of Rights that has ever been written. This Bill of Rights is not for one country, but for all countries. With the passion of artists we turn to this task, and let beauty, not political pragmatism, guide our hands, as we write!

There is a great scene in the play *Einstein and Picasso at the Lapin Agile* that captures our goal of writing together. The play takes place in a Paris bistro at the turn of the twentieth century. Picasso and Einstein are sitting in the bistro and a patron asks them what inspired them to achieve their breakthrough ideas in the fields of art and physics. They pause and quietly mull over the question. Then Einstein blurts out that theories must be "beautiful" and that the sun revolving around the Earth "is not beautiful enough." Then they have this conversation about beautiful ideas:

> PICASSO: So you're saying you bring a beautiful idea into being?
>
> EINSTEIN: Yes. We create a system and see if the facts can fit it.

PICASSO: So you're not just describing the world as it is?

EINSTEIN: No! We are creating a new way of looking at the world!

PICASSO: So you're saying you dream the impossible and put it into effect?

EINSTEIN: Exactly!

PICASSO: Brother!

EINSTEIN: Brother!

(Picasso and Einstein hug)[84]

And so it is with our international social order—"it's not beautiful enough." Of course, there is some beauty in our social order, just as there was beauty in art and formulas prior to Picasso and Einstein. But often—as is evident from holocausts, wars, even the minute-by-minute tragedies of children dying needlessly from lack of clean water, food, or decent health care—it is ugly. As Picasso and Einstein did, it is time at the turn of our new millennium for us to "dream the impossible and put it into effect." It is time to write a new social order that is more beautiful.

There is a major difference, however, between our writing a plan to restructure our social order and Picasso's breakthrough in art. Whereas a painting is best created by one person, a revision of our agreement to live together can best be written with widespread, international participation. A good comparison here is the development of computer code through open source programming. Many of the most powerful programs at use in the world today were posted for public contribution, just as 2048 is doing with its International Convention on Human Rights. People all over the world have contributed their thinking to build better programs. "The philosophy of open source is simple: when code can be modified and changed by many programmers, it evolves and improves."[85]

For this reason, while we let beauty guide us through the next four steps, we also need to share the 2048 path with others. In today's cacophony of information, awareness is power. Nothing is more important to the achievement of humanity's agreement to live together than an international awareness that such an agreement is underway and that everyone is encouraged to participate. Those with an audience, or with funds to provide for the infusion of the idea of 2048 into the consciousness of humanity, are asked to bring as many people as they can to join the path. Genuinely, the people and organizations who bring others to share the path to join the movement, are just as important, or more important, as the people who work on the specific language of articles in the International Convention. Through the ubiquitous Internet with its websites and social networking, there is nothing any person or government can do to stop the awakening of this awareness and the natural progression for our international community to take a common path together. I am not so naïve as to believe that the Internet cannot be limited, as it is in some countries, but events in Iran in 2009 have shown that it is impossible today to stop all communications from leaking out into the international community, including pictures. Yes, it remains true that relatively few people have most of the wealth and control of the media in the world, but that is changing. With the Internet they are losing their grip and we are gaining our minds.

In addition, many media leaders today have a following of viewers, listeners, and readers because they've developed trust among those who follow them. They are trusted to bring innovative ideas into the consciousness of hundreds of millions of people. These leaders, like Oprah Winfrey and Bono, have dramatically elevated the arts and letters through their own contributions and by inspiring millions of people to think and care about social change. Through accomplishments such as building schools and eliminating debt for impoverished countries, they set examples for what can be done. Through 2048, work such as theirs can expand into a social movement that harnesses the energy of people in all countries.

With beauty as our guide and inclusion as our goal, let's take a look at each of the four steps that we can take on the path together.

CHAPTER 12

Focus Together

Oscar Arias has brought the world together to focus on arms reduction and demilitarization

Confucius told us that "a journey of a thousand miles begins with a single step." This first step, to focus together, is the most important for 2048 because once it is taken other steps naturally follow. It is difficult to take this first step because of what it requires: *willpower.* To focus together takes the willpower to talk with others in your home town or in other countries about 2048. All social movements like 2048 are driven more by word of mouth than anything else. Unless we talk together and come up with a plan to do something, then we are little more than observers—aware of the folly of war, poverty, and environmental ruin, but allowing ourselves and our children to remain victims of it. Focus is when we decide to *do* something together.[86]

Eleanor's words on the death of Franklin Roosevelt inspire us to do something. She wrote, "A leader may chart the way, may point out the road to lasting peace, but ... many leaders and many peoples must do the building."[87] Her words applied well to Franklin, and now they apply well to her. Through 2048, people from all countries can focus together "to do the building."

The challenge is for each of us to join in to help do the building. A good place to begin is to become a member of 2048. You can easily join on the website. Membership is free, but a donation of $20.48 is requested. All members receive a newsletter three times a year, e-mail updates about events, and program developments. Those who donate $20.48 receive a copy of this book and a 2048 mug for coffee or tea. Although we need as many members as possible, let us not expect that every person, in every country, will participate. Humanity will have an agreement to live together when 1% of the people in all countries (approximately sixty-five million) have talked with one another about how an International Bill of Rights is being written and agreed to participate in 2048.

It is not that we do not want more than 1%, of course we do, but it's important that we not feel the enormity of reaching everyone. If 1% of humanity will focus together, and then carry out the following next three steps to *think together, write together,* and *decide together,* this will put sufficient pressure on governments to convince them to act. Many people within government support enforceable human rights, but they need to be able to show there is a popular movement to support their position. Finally governments will abide by the requirement of Article 28 of the Universal Declaration that "an international social order" be created to bring about "the full realization" of the rights in the Universal Declaration. 2048 is not asking for a new deal from governments; 2048 is insisting that governments keep the deal of the Universal Declaration!

How then do we persuade 1% of humanity to focus together? As crass as it may sound to some, we need to popularize 2048. We need the help of marketing professionals. Just as there are thousands of people with millions of dollars working tirelessly and spending lavishly to drum up popular support for the existing system of never-ending militarization, 2048 can also make its way into the public marketplace.

Our goal is not to convince people about 2048, but to find those with an existing shared interest in enforceable human rights, whatever their profession, whether it is cooking or international network television. This goal is timely because through social networking on Facebook, My Space, Twitter, and so on, within the span of a few moments millions of people can be focusing together.

As a result of these new technologies, those with a social network are in a powerful position. While this certainly includes celebrities with large followings, it also includes the millions of people who are using these new networking tools to connect with their friends and family to have thoughtful discussions, as well as to stay abreast of the latest news and entertainment. Social networking is empowering and capable of developing international trends such as 2048.

It is the *dialogue process* through social networking that is most essential. The Internet provides an opportunity to build a new kind of international understanding, not politician to politician, great person to great person, but citizen to citizen.[88] We can gather input from a wide range of scholars, organizations, and individuals, including those in less affluent countries, and do so in an enjoyable, lighthearted way. Changing our social order does not have to be a stuffy, weary exercise—that is certainly not the society we'll create when we're done!

The most valuable thing we can give is our *time.* The person who presents materials about 2048 at a meeting, or makes a comment on the website, has made the most essential contribution—he or she has given *time* and that is the first and most important step to focus together. People who take that step start a ripple that brings others to focus as well.

Given the requirements of everyday life, it is also important to recognize that focusing together is *not* a full-time job. I understand that many people are busy working to build a good community right in their own neighborhoods. I share these feelings. I have been a baseball coach for my boys and there are few things more satisfying than watching kids develop and have fun. The goal of 2048 is to complement these things, not replace them. Spreading the word can be done through conversation on the edges of our daily routine, whether at work or leisure.

Part of the difficulty of focusing together is the tension between constructing a new social order and living daily life within the existing one. Our daily lives, often including our paychecks, are the product of the ongoing plan to prepare for war. The influence of over *$1.4 trillion* a year in military spending is vast in scale. Millions of people, both inside and outside the military, arise each day to make weapons and to think about how to use them. These are mostly decent, hardworking people. We should not assume they will not support 2048.[89] They love their children and tend to their homes as do the millions of people working in nongovernmental organizations. People are not working to make trillions of dollars in weapons because they are evil. They are doing so because the leaders of our international community are still living by an outdated Roman maxim, "If you want peace, then prepare for war," and that is where the jobs and paychecks are.

With the understanding that we are reaching out to 1% of humanity, and that we want to popularize 2048 to reach them, we need to make it easy for people to focus together—even when they have little time. Let's consider some specific approaches about how we can focus together through philanthropy, education, business, and the arts.

Focus Through Philanthropy

If you are going to have a party, you need to tell people about it so that they can show up. The same is true for a social movement. People cannot focus together unless they learn that there is something to focus on. Philanthropy provides the means to inform people. Philanthropy does not make social movements, but it can facilitate them by giving them the means to grow. Given that there are tens of millions of people scattered throughout countries internationally who believe we are living within a flawed social order and who are willing to act to change it, philanthropy can reach them with the message that 2048 is something they can focus on with others to make that change. Word of mouth is essential to this end, including within the world of philanthropy. While the International Convention is a document that embodies humanity's written agreement, it is word of mouth that will bring people together to draft the document.

Philanthropy directed toward bringing people, organizations, and governments to focus together recognizes that since 2048 does not claim to have a perfect international bill of rights, the most important achievement 2048 makes is not the draft document itself, but the *process* that enables individuals, organizations, and governments to communicate together about how they can change that document or write their own. 2048, like the philanthropy supporting it, serves as a *facilitator.* The people, organizations, and governments who make the decision to work to draft an agreement to live together are the leaders.

Philanthropy plays a key role to bring people to focus together because it influences what people focus on. Often projects tend to follow funding. Presently almost all of the funds available are for a multitude of small fixes and cleaning up the by-product of a flawed social order; therefore, this is what most people and organizations do. On the other hand, if funds are are directed toward structural changes such as 2048, then people and organizations will work on those as well.

A few passages from the poem "An Ambulance or a Fence?", by Joseph Malins, dramatically captures the present situation.[90]

> 'Twas a dangerous cliff, as they freely confessed, Though to walk near its crest was so pleasant; But over its terrible edge there had slipped
>
> A duke and full many a peasant.
> So the people said something would have to be done,

But their projects did not at all tally;
Some said, 'Put a fence around the edge of the cliff,'
Some, 'An ambulance down in the valley.'

But the cry for the ambulance carried the day,
For it spread through the neighboring city;
A fence may be useful or not, it is true,
But the dwellers in highway and alley
Gave pounds or gave pence, not to put up a fence,
But an ambulance down in the valley.

Then an old sage remarked: 'It's a marvel to me
That people give far more attention
To repairing results than to stopping the cause,
When they'd much better aim at prevention.
Let us stop at its source all this mischief,' cried he,
'Come, neighbors and friends, let us rally;
If the cliff we will fence we might almost dispense
With the ambulance down in the valley.'

'Oh, he's a fanatic,' the others rejoined.
'Dispense with the ambulance? Never!
He'd dispense with all charities, too, if he could;
No! No! We'll support them forever.
Aren't we picking up folks just as fast as they fall?
And shall this man dictate to us? Shall he?

Why should people of sense stop to put up a fence,
While the ambulance works in the valley?

But a sensible few, who are practical too,
Will not bear with such nonsense much longer;
They believe that prevention is better than cure,
And their party will soon be the stronger.
Encourage them then, with your purse, voice, and pen,
And while other philanthropists dally,
They will scorn all pretense and put up a stout fence
On the cliff that hangs over the valley.

The International Bill of Rights being drafted by the 2048 Project is a stout fence. Many philanthropists will dally no longer and are adding their purse, voice, and pen to building this fence. However, just because a fence is under construction does not mean that we should stop building ambulances! Ambulances below are essential while a fence is under construction, and even after the fence is constructed there will always be a need for ambulances because no fence is perfect. However, by focusing together to construct a new agreement to live together, we can dramatically reduce the need for ambulances.

Courage is at the heart of changing from ambulances to a fence. Eleanor Roosevelt recognized this when she said,

> I wish you the courage to face yourselves and when you know what you really want to be and when you know what you really want to fight for, not in a war but in order to gain a peace, then I wish you imagination and understanding.[91]

Courage applies to the decision to build a fence when foundations have been funding ambulances. But it's not too late; both can be done. Bringing people to focus on a fence such as an International Bill of Rights can achieve the larger missions of foundations and individual philanthropists.

Focus Through Education

While word of mouth is essential to focusing together, it alone is not enough. We also need to systematically teach our children about the evolution of fundamental human rights and the ongoing movement to make human rights enforceable in all countries. The Universal Declaration of Human Rights proclaims that "every individual and every organ of society shall strive by teaching and education to promote the rights and freedoms in the UDHR." *Every* student in *every* school in *every* country needs to be taught about the rights that we all share—simply by being human—regardless of nationality, race, wealth, or gender. 2048 has developed a curriculum to provide some of the human rights education the Universal Declaration requires. The curriculum is designed for Human Rights Day, December 10th, and it is created to be available internationally each year.

Human Rights Day has been celebrated in many countries since 1950. The goal for Human Rights Day is to have secondary school and university students in all countries focus together on the same day using identical materials translated into many languages. In 2009 there were approximately 900 million students between the ages of 15 and 25 worldwide. 2048 aspires to one day have all high school and university students in all countries learn, on the same day, about rights they all share.

To this end, the 2048 Human Rights Day curriculum provides a film made by students for students depicting the evolution of human rights and a lesson plan for teachers to use in guiding students through discussion.[92] These educational materials are available on the 2048 website, so any teacher may readily participate by merely going to the website. Those teachers who lack Internet access are mailed the materials free of charge by 2048. After seeing the film, and having a discussion in class, students are asked to be "drafters," similar to the drafters who wrote the Universal Declaration, and to make a comment on the 2048 website about the draft International Convention. By thinking as drafters, they learn to be leaders because they have to choose which rights to include in the document and think about the ramifications of their selection. For teachers who want their students to think even more deeply, this book is available for free, or at a discount, if it will be used in the classroom.

In sum, students learn about a common bond of human rights that exists in our international community. This bond is essential for the realization of rights and respect for them. Education plays an important role in the formation of character. As John Locke wrote in *Some Thoughts Concerning Education,* "Of all the men, nine parts out of ten of what they are, good or evil, useful or not, is determined by their education."[93] People must be aware of their rights in order to exercise them. And when they are taught that these are rights we *share,* they understand their duty to respect the rights of others. In this way, over time, rights become common values enforced through mutual respect as well as through courts.

Focus Through Business

Business requires focus as well. Anyone who has ever tried to start a small business, or run a large one, knows that in a capitalistic economy business is full of risks and challenges, as it should be. When a business loses focus, and stops striving for improvement, it deteriorates. The same is true for the evolution of rights.

Looking ahead, one emerging trend is regulation of globalization. While globalization has many accomplishments it is also true that harm to workers, the environment, and society at large can occur when one business engages in exploitative practices to outcompete another. For example, it can be a cost savings for a company to use inexpensive child labor even though that child should be in school. When one company does so, it puts pressure on other companies to do the same. If they do not, they will lose market share because their products will cost more than the same products made with child labor.

Since the heart of business is survival, the result is a "race to the bottom." A downward spiral occurs whereby businesses compete with one another to make their product with the cheapest child labor, regardless of the negative social consequences. The race to the bottom is further exacerbated when some countries have fewer protections for labor and the environment than others. When this happens, large companies flock to these countries to make their products. This puts those countries with higher environmental and labor protection at a disadvantage. As Richard Falk, one of the foremost authorities on international human rights, has explained:

> Until these global market forces can be regulated on the basis of human, and environmental, priorities, the dynamics of trade, investment, and growth are likely to gravely jeopardize the mission of human rights to protect those who are most at risk economically, socially, politically, and culturally.[94]

A new bottom line of protection for labor and the environment is needed in all countries to prevent this race to the bottom from sinking too far.

Since capitalism is the prevailing international economic model, we must address its weaknesses as well as enjoy its strengths. Focusing together on 2048 is also well suited for farsighted business leaders.

Because of the demands of consumers and shareholders, and because people in business share social and environmental concerns, there is growing support for businesses to adopt voluntary codes of conduct. These codes often include protections for labor and the environment. As we discussed in Chapter 2, the problem, however, is that once responsible companies voluntarily adopt codes of conduct, they are placed at a competitive disadvantage with the unscrupulous companies that do not adopt similar codes.[95] To prevent this disparity, it is in the financial interest of companies that have adopted voluntary codes of conduct to focus together on an International Convention because it will force their competitors to compete at their level.

The financial incentive for for-profit businesses to support an International Convention provides a great opportunity for them to collaborate with nonprofit organizations. By focusing together on an International Convention, for-profits and nonprofits can increase their power and influence to accomplish their respective goals. In addition, given the considerable influence that they both have with legislative bodies, they can persuade governments to participate as well.

Focus Through the Arts

While education can teach, and business can lead, the arts can inspire us to focus together. We have all been stirred by a song, a poem, or a painting. It is something we share in common. Those who sing, act, write, and paint can bring us to focus together regardless of our country, race, sex, or profession. They have our ears, eyes, minds, and often our hearts. Artists, however, as with nonprofit and for-profit businesses, need something on which to focus. The draft International Convention on Human Rights is a palette. The written document, as with a painting, is measured by what is most beautiful, not by what is most politically acceptable. The words in the document reflect feelings that will become legal rights.

Artists, including actors and authors who move us with a gesture or a word, have the power to bring much of humanity to focus together on 2048. It is fitting that artists bring us to focus together. Artists have the power to inspire us to act for ourselves instead of relying on others, and they have the personal power and insight to make significant contributions regarding the content of the International Convention as well.[96]

Writing a social contract requires a social movement. Artists can inspire millions of people across all borders and lead us to write our agreement about how we will live together in our international community. Bono and the band U2 have demonstrated this power by speaking out early on for the release of Nelson Mandela and by displaying the Universal Declaration of Human Rights on a giant screen during their tour in 2006. Moreover, art is a satisfying and enjoyable way to focus together. Norman Rockwell showed through his paintings depicting the Four Freedoms that they can be captured in a light-hearted yet meaningful manner.

The International Convention is art—a composition by humanity, for humanity. A sense of purpose and satisfaction resides within the act of millions of people and organizations focusing together to create a work of art. It is all the more beautiful because the document can be enforced in courts of law. Our courtrooms will be "galleries" for our living, evolving document.

Focusing Together Brings Cooperation

Focusing together on 2048 also encourages us to live together. The present plan to prepare for war incessantly puts millions of people internationally against one another. It is a negative mindset. In contrast, 2048 prepares people to cooperate with one another, and is uplifting. Most people can recall a feeling of well-being when they have engaged with others in a collective endeavor. We remember a sense of community, friendship, and teamwork. One example humanity has witnessed repeatedly over the past fifty years is the emergence of peaceful social movements based on cooperation that have stirred people's hearts and minds and led to social change. Dr. Martin Luther King, Jr. is a good example. Much of his work was built on principles learned from Gandhi in India. Dr. King went to India to study Gandhi's teachings before he, along with many others, embarked on the American Civil Rights Movement. Through focusing together, 2048 fosters this type of international shared insight and inspiration.

The people marching with Gandhi shared feelings of cooperation and camaraderie that are quintessential in human character. Peacefully, but with determination, they walked headfirst into the opposition, literally—no matter how savage the blows. This sense of cooperation and camaraderie is universal as can be seen during other times of social transformation. The crumbling of the Berlin Wall and the fall of apartheid in South Africa are good examples. Divisive walls built today will deteriorate tomorrow. The human spirit yearns to integrate, not separate.

The social contract we focus on today becomes our way of life tomorrow. This is how social movements develop, with a sense of purpose combined with cooperation. The two together make the difference between a fleeting movement versus a long-term effort. So with the inspiration and support of teachers, businesspeople and artists, and as a cooperative effort, let us focus together to take our next steps to think, write, and decide together.

CHAPTER 13

Think Together

P.C. Chang was a philosopher who led the drafters of the Universal Declaration of Human Rights to think together

Once we have the will to focus together on an International Convention on Human Rights, then we can think together about what is the best wording for the Convention. Thinking together requires each of us—regardless of race, wealth, nationality, or profession—to set aside our separate egos and biases so we can concentrate on drafting the best possible set of fundamental rights for all, not just for ourselves. To do this, we need to start with a common frame of mind. We do so by considering an "optimum" set of fundamental human rights. We ask: "What is the optimum wording for an International Convention on Human Rights?"

Thinking Together About Our Optimum Society

As we think together about what is optimum, we are *not* limiting ourselves to what leaders will agree to. One of the most pernicious and intransigent sentiments within the international human rights community is that we should think about fundamental rights in terms of what governments will accept, rather than what is best for the people. The result is that much of the time we have not even thought through what is optimum, so we don't know where we should be heading or how we should get there.

What the president of a nation, the president of a university, or the president of a large international company or union will accept or reject is *never* determinative. We are thinking together about what *we* choose for our social contract, not what leaders will allow us to select. Of course, the thoughts of presidents are valuable, but no more so than those of the staff, teachers, or clerks who work for them. Anyone who believes in equality cannot conclude otherwise. Each person has an equal say regarding the content of our social contract.

So when we say we are "thinking together," we mean that we are "investigating together" into what an optimal list of rights in an International Convention would be. We do not know; we will never know perfectly. We will, however, gain insight through our inquiry. By using what is optimum as our guide, we are concentrating on the weight of the idea, not the identity of the person, organization, or institution. The draft International Convention is not the product of any particular institution—it is a product of all the individuals, organizations, and institutions who participate.

One of the key purposes of 2048 is to amass a body of thinking based on what is optimum rather than what is politically possible. 2048 is unafraid to think about things as they might be as well as the way they are. A skeptic will say, "So what if we think together about what is optimum; we will not agree. We are too culturally different to reach any agreement." To this, the answer is "Let's see." As was discussed in Chapter 5 on freedom of religion, Gandhi found otherwise. He found that "the deeper that he went, the more there was in common." So let us research deeply. Let us think together about what is optimum with international input from all but dependence on none—on an equal basis. When we do, it is likely that there will still be issues about which there is too much disparity to reach agreement. It is also possible, however, that we will find that the deeper we go, particularly if we obtain broad-based input from thousands of individuals and organizations from many nations, the more we will find that "we have in common"—at least enough to draft and ratify an International Convention on Human Rights by the year 2048.

Next the skeptic will say, "It is nice to think about what is optimum, but that is unrealistic, so why bother?" This is the most egregious of criticisms. It rests on the presumption that one view, "If we wish for peace, then we must prepare for war" is "realistic"—all else is unreal and unworthy of consideration. This, we are told, is "realpolitik." Our answer to this closed-mindedness was provided by Robert Kennedy. He said, "Some men see things as they are and question why? I dream things that never were and say, why not?"[97] Robert's words reflect the thinking of many great leaders spanning all countries and all professions who have dared to think about how things might be rather than accept the way they are.[98]

One example is Nicolaus Copernicus. For centuries, "reality," as declared by the pope, was that the Earth was the "fixed" center of the universe with the sun, planets, and stars moving around it. Copernicus disproved this in his book, *On the Revolutions of the Celestial Spheres,* which out of fear he did not allow to be published during his life. Another example is when Einstein developed his theories of relativity in 1905 and 1915. At that time Newtonian principles were taken as "fact." But if Einstein was right, then Newton was wrong; Einstein was right.

Considering how Copernicus and Einstein challenged what was accepted as "reality," and were proven correct, it is wise also to question the "fact" of war and poverty as inherent parts of our social order. Rousseau did this with his refusal to accept the "reality" of his time that monarchs were divinely chosen by God. Instead, he detached himself from the social order of the time and came up with his own theory. These lessons teach that by questioning reality we may come closer to it. Each new reality is a result of dreams of what might be.

Even though we are thinking about what is optimum, we do not discard our human traits. Rather, as Rousseau said, "We act by considering human beings as they are and laws as they might be." Therefore, with 2048 we think about what is optimum and then compare that with what we have. As Copernicus did with astronomy, we will look at our "fixed" social order and see if there is another order that is in better harmony with humanity—just as rotation about the sun was in better harmony with the universe. There is nothing new about this approach of reevaluation; it has already proved to lead to breakthroughs. Businesses, if they wish to stay in business, go through this process of reassessment and restructuring all the time. Many wise people do as well.

Also, as we think about what is optimum, let us strive for perfection, but not expect it. As Eleanor Roosevelt said, "The quest for human rights is a fulfilling, yet never fulfilled endeavor." Our optimum list need not be perfect because there will be more lists to follow. An International Convention on Human Rights will be an important advancement to make the rights in the Universal Declaration of Human Rights, as well as the twin Covenants on human rights and other U.N. documents, "fully realized" as they will become legally enforceable. Nevertheless, over time, perhaps a long time, the International Convention will have to be rewritten. Our social contract is an ongoing, never-ending evolutionary process, so the evolution of our documents embedding that contract must be ongoing and never-ending as well.

With the understanding that our standard is what is optimum rather than what is perfect, we now will think together about the general contours of a list of fundamental rights to be included within an International Convention on Human Rights.

Philosophical Foundation for Thinking Together

Given our goal of an optimum list, how do we select what to include in the list? Here, fortunately, philosophy provides guidance for how our international community can think together about a list of rights for an International Bill of Rights. One theory in particular, John Rawls's *Theory of Justice,* is a helpful guide for how we can think together about a list of fundamental rights.

Rawls assists us to prepare a list of fundamental rights from a shared perspective. That is, each of us in our homes, offices, schools, factories, or wherever else we might be when we are contemplating this list of rights, will attempt to prepare the list from a similar state of mind. Doing so does not mean that we will all reach the same result, but that we will do the best we can to engage in the same task.

The reason we want everyone in our international community to think together from a similar perspective is because the ultimate outcome of the next two steps, to write and to decide together, will produce documents that will apply to everyone in our international community. As broad a base of humanity as possible should think about the content of an International Convention on Human Rights so that we all feel comfortable with the document created. In addition, those who help create an International Convention through direct participation will feel a special kinship with it, and be more inclined to respect the rights within that document.

Rawls has three books for us to consider as we prepare a list of fundamental rights: *A Theory of Justice,*[99] *Political Liberalism,*[100] and *The Law of Peoples.*[101] This trilogy provides a framework to draft an International Bill of Rights. As we apply philosophy here, our goal is to be fair. That is, while it is impossible to completely eliminate bias and prejudice, we will try to remove this taint when we think together about a list of rights. To facilitate this, I'm admittedly applying a summary view of Rawls's theory to facilitate our thinking together.

Rawls offers an approach we can use to reduce our bias and prejudice when we are selecting a list of rights. He uses what he calls a "veil of ignorance." The veil of ignorance is a voluntary filter that we apply to ourselves as best we can when we begin to think about a list of rights. According to Rawls, the idea of the veil of ignorance is that "as people pick a list of rights, no one knows his place in society, his class position or social status."[102]

What this means is that as we think together about rights, we assume that we do not know what country we are a citizen of, how much wealth we and our family have, or what race, sex, or religion we are. We do know, however, that in the present social order there is racial, gender, and religious prejudice, and that there are gross economic disparities, including that two-thirds of humanity, four billion people, are living on less than $4.00 a day. According to the World Bank, almost half of the world's people—2.8 billion—live on less than $2.00 a day.[103] In short, we try to block out our existing individual position in our present social order, but are still aware of the contours of that order.

Fundamentally, the voluntary application of the veil gives us the ability to put ourselves into the shoes of others. Think of it this way: Imagine that you are creating a social order for our international community whereby you could instantly be born into any town, city or nation. Then pick your list of rights that applies to all towns, cities and nations. If we truly long for justice and want to enforce universal human rights, this is a way to think together to achieve that goal.

The result of voluntarily applying the veil of ignorance is that we select rights that work for all and when we do so we create a world that works for all. What works for all, also works for each of us. Since behind the veil we do not know our place in society, we are careful to make sure our rights are protected under any circumstances. When we think together in this way, universal rights are established that protect each of us, and we know that each of us, in every town, city, and nation will live a decent life based upon fundamental human rights.

Furthermore, by placing ourselves behind a veil of ignorance where we ignore our race, sex, social status, and other characteristics, we are less likely to select rights that prejudice us against race or sex because there is no incentive in doing so. As Rawls explains, under the veil no one will select prejudicial rights such as different castes because "no one can tell whether such principles would be to his advantage."[104] Often the true purpose of prejudice is to perpetuate position and power. Asking people to apply the veil and then make a list in writing exposes self-serving reasons for perpetuating personal power and position over others.

Of course, even when people are sincere in their attempt to apply the veil, it is impossible to do so completely, as each of us has biases built deeply into our psyche that effectively block them. But it does not matter that we are unable to apply the veil perfectly. Although each of us as human beings has accumulated biases and prejudices, and it would be dishonest to claim otherwise, or to assume that we can voluntarily remove all bias and prejudice from our thinking, what is important is that *we try.* We may not succeed completely; however, we can consciously curb our biases and prejudice by voluntarily applying the veil, and thus create a better list than we would have otherwise.

Thinking Together Across Generations

There is more than one reason we have chosen 2048 as the date for the realization of rights in the Universal Declaration. The first, as you know, is that 2048 is the 100th anniversary of the Universal Declaration. Another is that a forty-year outlook crosses generational lines. Just as it is not easy to apply the veil of ignorance voluntarily, it is not easy for us to think beyond our own lives. We are preoccupied with ourselves. If, however, we accept this tendency toward self-centeredness, then we may transcend it and begin to think of others, particularly our children and even our grandchildren.

And, with or without children, there is another force at work: most of us want to leave a mark. We want to give as well as take during the time of our existence. A major drive of philanthropy is this desire to give back. Thinking together across generations gives us all an opportunity to leave a lasting impact that survives us. Through 2048 each of us may be only a small part of a movement, but it is a part of something *big.* When we think together we can accomplish something grander than any of us could accomplish individually.

Grand thinking is appropriate at this point in time. Many people start foundations and nonprofits based on this desire to leave a mark, a legacy, an imprint on the humanity of which they are part. Without these efforts, the world would be even worse off than it is, and I genuinely admire and applaud them. But let's also be honest and admit that our cross-generational imprint as an international community is that we are on a path to leave a world for future generations that is despoiled. Unfortunately, it is difficult for parents today to claim that we "left the world better than we found it." Given this fact, it makes sense that we think together about a grand plan to be implemented over forty years to reverse this trend.

The ultimate goal is to keep an open mind as we reassess our situation and design an International Convention. The financier and author, George Soros, has written persuasively about the need for reassessment at the societal level. In describing what he calls an "open society," he stresses the following: "We must treat our beliefs as provisionally true while keeping them open to constant reexamination. This is the foundation principle of an open society."[105] Like an open society, 2048 is based on the recognition that people have divergent views and interests and nobody is in possession of the ultimate truth. Therefore, we approach the next two steps of writing together and deciding together with an open mind and a philosophical perspective in which we think about others as well as ourselves.

CHAPTER 14

Write Together

Tim Berners-Lee, the founder of the World Wide Web that runs on the Internet and enables humanity to write an International Bill of Rights together

Once people and organizations have agreed to focus together and think together, the next step is to write together. At first it might seem that this step is fairly simple. After all, as we have seen from our discussion thus far, if we have the will to focus together and have thought together about an optimum list of fundamental rights, then we should be able just to write down the list. Unfortunately, while our progress so far is helpful, it's not that easy.

Even with the focus of an open mind and the philosophical guidance of the veil of ignorance with which to draft an optimum document, we are incapable of *verbally* telling one another in our international community about a list of fundamental rights without its becoming a jumble. A version of the game, Telephone, is played by children in many languages. A group of children sit in a circle. One child starts by telling a story to the person next to him or her, and the story is passed around from one to another until it makes its way back to the start. Usually, the final story that emerges is much different from the story that started and everyone has a good laugh.

There is a solution to this problem—it is writing. We can write down our draft International Convention so that we can pass it around and rewrite it as we collect comments. In this way, we can see when and where the document has changed, and why. It is essential that we follow this process because we communicate in so many languages. Only if we write comments down and have good translations can we hope to have a clear understanding of the content of the Convention.

Part of the 2048 mission is to provide a *process* for people, internationally, to write together. Some people may feel that they lack the expertise to write. Don't worry, expertise is not needed. The will to write is more important than the expertise. You do not need to be a lawyer or a scholar to read and comment on the International Convention. Of course, judges and lawyers have a useful role. Their insights are valuable since they work with the interpretation and enforcement of documents regularly, but no human rights document would be optimum if it were written only by judges and lawyers. A variety of backgrounds leads to a variety of insights. It is from variety that the best ideas can be culled and combined.

Since the more diverse the input, the better the output, the core of 2048 is its website. A primary goal of 2048 is to have as many people as possible make comments about what should be on the canvas of the document. The question, then, is not who should contribute to the canvas—we know the answer—it is everyone. The question is what canvas is large enough for everyone? Fortunately, an answer to that question has emerged in the past ten years: the Internet.

Drafting Through Dialogue

The Internet gives us the ability to collect, cull, and combine international input with the use of the website www.2048.berkeley.edu and social networking tools. The use of a website and social networking for humanity to reach an agreement to live together will be one of the greatest achievements of the Internet over the coming years. The 2048 website is designed with the following simple premise: All of us, internationally, are writing together. Anyone can post a comment. It can be one word, or 10,000 words—we call this "drafting through dialogue."

The key is that drafting through dialogue is a discussion *in writing.* This includes students in high school classrooms with their teachers on Human Rights Day, professors at universities teaching human rights courses, foundations and philanthropists, business leaders with their staffs, activists working to build justice and fairness into globalization, and political representatives working toward security for their constituents. It cannot be otherwise because we are drafting a social contract. It applies to us all, so we *all* should participate. A similar approach is being taken with the National Human Rights Consultation website for Australia.[106] The goal of the consultation is "to seek a range of views from across Australia about the protection and promotion of human rights." 2048 has the same objective, except at an international rather than a domestic level.

The pen is indeed mightier than the sword, but it is more difficult to get someone to pick one up; therefore, 2048 makes participation simple. The heart of the website is the *submission of ideas.* You don't need to pay, nor do you need to sign in—you can even leave an anonymous comment if you prefer. It is collective writing; therefore the result is a collective consciousness embodied in a document—the substance of our social contract for all to see, enjoy, and enforce.

One of the best aspects of "drafting through dialogue" is that it advances scholarly research while simultaneously allowing for public comment. The method for drafting the International Convention draws on the experience of similar efforts undertaken by the International Law Association, however, 2048 adds the public at large. Whether the comment is being made by a scholar or a member of the general public, the objective is the same: to collect comments about the potential wording of an International Convention, including suggestions for the *deletion* of an existing article, the *modification* of the wording of an existing article, or the *addition* of a new article.

"Reporters," people who work for 2048 and are willing to consider all comments with the help of staff, are responsible for reviewing all comments made about the International Convention.[107] Changes made to the draft International Convention as a result of insights from comments are carefully recorded with an entry on the website containing a subject heading "Text Change." No changes are made to the draft Convention that are not recorded on the website, including reference to the comment that was the catalyst for the change. Reporters may also make changes on their own; however, as with all other comments, any new text inserted by the reporters must be explained on the website. By following this procedure, there is a written history regarding the evolution of the document.

All comments are stored for posterity. They are saved through an ongoing archiving process. One reason comments are saved is to see where they lead. The website provides a platform where gradual support, or opposition, to a proposed right can accumulate. Writers can come back to their comments and build on them, or others may make a comment, thereby sparking a dialogue with the writer of the original comment. In this manner, comments are an ongoing dialogue process. This process is called *brainstorming.* Brainstorming involves throwing ideas out in an open, supportive environment with the understanding that not every idea will be incorporated; however, we benefit from collecting as many ideas as possible, including comments containing strong opposition to the entire process.

In this spirit, comments may be strong, but should not be disrespectful or condescending. Every comment is welcome in the 2048 marketplace of ideas. One of the beauties of the written word is that it can be pondered. It sits on the page to be measured, remeasured, and questioned anew. There may even be second thoughts about a comment. We are writing together in the tradition of Socratic dialogue. We exchange and combine thoughts with the goal of reaching ever-higher levels of insight and understanding. Furthermore, comments are not expected to be flashes of brilliance, although they may be. More often the picture that is formed through comments is closer to "connect the dots," where each connection brings out the picture with more clarity.

Writing Comments

There are two types of comments that can be made about the International Convention on the 2048 website, *general* and *specific.* General comments are intended for any comment of a general nature. For example, you might comment on whether the International Convention is a good or a bad idea, as well as who might participate, and why.

In addition to general comments, participants may post a specific comment on an article, or even an issue within an article, for the Convention. As with general comments, specific comments are intended for brainstorming. The website is designed so that any of the articles in the draft International Convention can be selected, and a comment can be made about that specific article. If the individual or organization posting a comment concludes that there needs to be a modification of the wording to a specific article, then they are asked to provide suggested new wording. Of course, they may also suggest what wording needs to be removed. Everyone is a drafter and all comments go through the same review process.

Because people are curious about what others have to say, the website includes the ability to search comments by the author's name, and also by topic, so that if one is researching a particular field like free speech or education one can easily find a wealth of resources at one's fingertips, including papers, articles, and books. In this way the 2048 website is a valuable resource center as well as a working site for drafting the International Convention.

In addition to collecting comments on the website, 2048 also seeks input through correspondence, conferences, magazine articles, radio and television interviews, and other means. Every single comment, no matter how positive or negative, or how it is collected, furthers the success of 2048. *Success lies in process.* No one knows for sure what the exact text of the International Convention will be, and widespread input is the only way to find out. Writing together is also a physical process. Many people working together simultaneously toward a common goal create connections.

While holding hands is different from typing on keyboards, a remarkable event occurred where two million people joined hands across 400 miles (600 kilometers) of roadway through Estonia, Latvia, and Lithuania. They parked their cars and formed a human chain. So too, as each of us simultaneously takes up a keyboard or picks up a pen, we link together the hands and minds of millions of people. As was the case in Estonia, where, despite the efforts of authorities to break the chain, it endured, 2048 linkages cannot easily be pulled apart either.

Finally, not only individuals are encouraged to make comments; organizations are encouraged to comment as well. Many organizations have already done extensive research on human rights issues. It is our hope that they will submit their research to 2048 as a contribution to drafting through dialogue. In this manner, a wealth of information can be stored in a single location, allowing for focus and deliberation. The comment process is easy and inclusive. Here are a couple of examples to see how it works.

Students and Scholars Writing Together

Earlier we discussed how students and scholars internationally can focus together for Human Rights Day. Now we will discuss how they can write together. The Human Rights Day curriculum on the 2048 website combines focus and writing. After students have studied human rights documents, seen a film, and engaged in discussion with their teachers and classmates on December 10, they are asked to contribute their thoughts about an international convention on the 2048 website. This is not a simulation, as is so often the case with classroom projects. Students are participating in the actual creation of an International Convention on Human Rights that can be enforced in the courts of all countries. Student comments are reviewed by the reporters in the same manner as all other comments.

Students can also work with their teachers to develop more lengthy comments into papers, either as part of their teachers' research or as research they do on their own for course credit. A methodology has been developed at 2048 to give students and professors internationally the opportunity to write a twenty-page paper for the website. Papers may be longer or shorter than twenty pages, but an effort is being made to develop a standard format to maintain some uniformity. There are three types of twenty-page papers: *Country, General,* and *Article.*

Country papers are designed to provide a wealth of human rights information about a country and to assess to what extent existing law in a particular country is compatible with the articles of the draft International Convention. To make this determination, the country's own Bill of Rights is studied, along with the international human rights treaties that the country has signed. This collection of information is put onto the website on a home page for each country which can easily be opened from the map on the 2048 "resources" page. Country papers provide a valuable comparison of the existing law in the country being reviewed with the text of the International Convention, to see what they have in common and where there are differences.

General papers are designed to discuss general ideas such as the pros and cons of 2048, or how the drafting process could be improved. They may also plumb issues such as the application of John Rawls's *Theory of Justice* as a guide to think together. Professors and scholars in any discipline may share their ideas through general essays. These essays may be about any topic related to 2048.

Article papers are designed to discuss a particular article in the International Convention, or even one issue within an article. For example, someone might write about the right to education, either in favor or against, or perhaps to explain how such a right would work in practice.

As with Human Rights Day, one of the key purposes of the papers is to stimulate students and their professors to research deeply (and sometimes together) the evolution of rights. To further this interaction, 2048 has created "digital internships" whereby students at universities internationally can work on 2048 as volunteers or receive course credit as part of their studies. There are many people thinking deeply and writing about human rights. These three types of essays give them the opportunity to share their thoughts. The intent of papers, like comments, is an international collective written embodiment of our social contract. Papers, articles, and books provide an explanation for the chosen wording of the International Convention. While they will not, and should not, be controlling over future judicial decisions interpreting the International Convention, it is hoped they will be helpful for providing some insight into original intent.

In Chapter 12, I recited a poem titled "An Ambulance or a Fence?" The 2048 papers, articles and books are all boards to build the fence. The size of the fence is the social science equivalent of the Great

Wall of China. Each day thousands of professors, students, musicians, authors, and others talk, sing, and write about human rights. These thoughts are also boards to be put on the 2048 fence. We cannot continue to leave these boards scattered about the cliff wondering why they are not stopping more bodies from going over the cliff. We need to gather these boards and put them on the fence.

As we write together, why not accept an intellectual challenge as demanding as the physical challenge of the Great Wall of China? The intellectual evolution of humanity is just as deep and profound as the physical evolution of it. Gandhi said, "What a man thinks about, he becomes." If true, then if we think about the Five Freedoms, that is what we will become: free. Let us combine the written pieces of our thinking together. There is strength in the consolidation of our work. We have something to learn from the business community which often combines to increase power. Too much of the thoughtful, scholarly writing on human rights is being written for the eyes of the few rather than the many. Instead of being included within the mainstream of our social order, much writing on human rights is often relegated to the periphery. Enough dancing on the periphery, let's move to the center!

Globalization is bringing about a concentration of wealth and power. It will take a concentration of progressive organizations and individuals to temper the existing trend. As George Soros has explained,

"The development of international institutions has not kept pace with the development of international financial markets, and our political arrangements have lagged behind the globalization of the economy."[108] To remedy this situation, Soros states that it is his mission is "to reform and strengthen our international institutions and create new ones where necessary to address social concerns that have fueled the current discontent."[109] This is *exactly* what 2048 is doing. 2048 facilitates writing together to strengthen existing transnational judicial institutions and to create a new judicial institution, an International Court of Human Rights that can "address social concerns that have fueled the current discontent."

The 2048 broad-based affiliation to write together can be seen on the left and right columns of the 2048 website. Affiliated universities and nongovernmental organizations have equal stature. *Any* university, for-profit, or nonprofit organization is welcome to join either of these lists. There is no hierarchy or litmus test. All universities and business organizations are listed in alphabetical order. As always, the weight of their contribution is the weight of their ideas. Grassroots organizations and movements are welcome on these lists as well. Many grassroots organizers recognize that protests are a valuable way to make voices heard and to gain attention, but they also realize that protests alone are often not sufficient to effectuate change. It helps to have something in writing to point to, and 2048 provides this. A document is something we can hold up and say, "Here is something we are *for!"*

Writing Together with the United Nations

Even though the end result of the 2048 process is a Convention that is enforceable in courts *outside* of the United Nations, just as the European Court of Human Rights and the International Criminal Court are *outside* of the United Nations, the drafting of an International Convention on Human Rights would benefit greatly from writing together with a "working group" created by the Human Rights Council at the United Nations. Eleanor Roosevelt chaired a working group to draft the Universal Declaration of Human Rights. The idea of the original working group for the Universal Declaration was similar to that of 2048, to collect a broad base of input to decide what rights should be included in the Universal Declaration.[110]

A parallel development by the 2048 Project and the United Nations Working Group to draft an International Convention could proceed as a collaborative effort. In addition, given the political pressures at the United Nations, the 2048 document can serve as a check to ensure that the focus is on what is optimal rather than what is politically acceptable. To this end, while an International Convention is being drafted as a 2048 document, at the same time, an International Convention should be prepared by a working group of the United Nations Human Rights Council. The time is right for the new Human Rights Council in Geneva (the successor to the Commission on Human Rights), to apply the mandate of Article 28 of the Universal Declaration and create a new working group, again comprising representatives of many nations, to draft an International Convention. As with the 2048 draft, the Human Rights Council draft can be a codification of many documents into a single document.

As is being done now by 2048, the new Human Rights Council Working Group should proceed with the goal of taking the rights in the Universal Declaration, including economic and social rights, and combining them with the legal process of the European Convention to create a new International Convention with an International Court of Human Rights. The Convention should be written with the intention that it will be enforceable in the courts of all countries, just as the European Convention is enforceable in the courts of 47 countries.

In addition to a new working group created by the U.N. Human Rights Council, another draft of an International Convention on Human Rights should be prepared by the International Law Commission (ILC).[111] The ILC was established in 1948, the same year as the creation of the Universal Declaration. The International Law Commission's mandate is the progressive development and codification of international law.[112] It would be a fitting 100th anniversary of the International Law Commission, along with the

100th anniversary of the Universal Declaration, to prepare a codification of human rights law into a single document enforceable in the courts of all countries. 2048 is initiating this process so that the ILC will have a considerable amount of thinking at its fingertips when it joins in.

The progress of the Human Rights Council Working Group and the International Law Commission, as with 2048, should be completely transparent. This way each will keep the other honest. The refrain for all three should be, "put it in writing," and all three should proceed with Internet websites so that there is open public scrutiny with respect to the selection of wording for the various articles. This transparency is essential both for honesty and to create a historical record that can be considered later when an International Convention is being interpreted through court decisions.

The three parallel websites will also provide fertile ground for competition in the "marketplace of ideas." The competition of ideas between the 2048 draft—the Human Rights Council Working Group draft—and the International Law Commission draft will test the reasoning of each, in writing, and facilitate an outcome that will be even stronger than could be produced by one without the other. Others may also participate in this healthy competition such as the Agenda for Human Rights,[113] a Swiss government initiative launched on the sixtieth anniversary of the Universal Declaration which has called for a World Court of

Human Rights. The Project for International Courts and Tribunals (PICT) also has a well established expertise that can be valuable for providing critique of the various drafts and it could also offer a draft of its own.[114] Competition, with collaboration, will bring the day when there is a codification into an International Bill of Rights, embodied in a single document that can be enforced in the courts of all countries!

Now that we have used our focus and thinking together to write together, it is time to decide together. We now turn to this final step.

CHAPTER 15

Decide Together

Dag Hammarskjold, the second Secretary-General for the United Nations, was a strong advocate for institutions to make human rights fully realized for people in all countries

Once we have taken the first three steps, the last step of deciding together is primarily to implement what we have done. Our focus, thinking, and writing have created a draft document of such substance and authenticity that it is ready for implementation. Having followed Gandhi, while acknowledging differences we will also have found "what we have in common."

It is important that we do not jump too quickly to try to decide together. This is not to say that we should not have a specific timetable, and 2048 provides one, but it should span many years so that there is sufficient time for the process of focusing, thinking, and writing together to grow and develop. It is important to go through a series of drafts. By being patient and thorough, when we act as an international community to decide together, we will have a substantial body of work about which we feel confident. Then we can meet in Rome to decide together.

Decide Together in Rome

Rome would be a good place to meet because humanity has already walked the path to this city several times to reach transnational agreements. The European Convention on Human Rights was created by a treaty passed in Rome in 1953. More recently, in 1998, the International Criminal Court was created by a treaty agreement in Rome. Rome has the historical precedent to be where the turning point for humanity ends and a new era of peace and prosperity begins.

It is at the juncture of deciding together where all of our meticulous preparation will bear fruit. Every comment from a student in a class using the 2048 Human Rights Day curriculum, every twenty-page essay submitted by a scholar on a specific article, every video of a conference held by the 2048 Project, every name of every university and organization that has become a participant in the process—these will all be placed on the table before the representatives of all countries when they convene in Rome.

While the full weight of all this work will be put before all countries, it is foreseeable that there will be those in power who will try to resist the Five Freedoms from becoming universally enforceable. Some will resist the work that has been done because it will be clear that the document being created will be enforceable in the courts of *all* countries. Unlike the case with some previous documents, government leaders cannot merely agree to the International Convention and then ignore it—courts will issue orders against them if they violate the rights in the International Convention.

Even if there is some opposition, humanity will be prepared for this moment because we will have used the outstanding technology we now have, the Internet, to put all of our thinking into writing. When we set the International Convention on the table in Rome it will be supported by enough documents to fill every square inch of the massive room in which the table sits. Thankfully, these documents will be on discs and by that time, probably one single disc. It will be a very powerful disc. On it will be the collective thinking of humanity about how we can live together.

Because of the deliberative process utilized to prepare that disc, it will not be an inspirational statement or a plea to leaders that they do something—it will be the social contract that governs them, and it will join us into one international community.[115] The content of such a disc is not threatening because government leaders, along with everyone else, will have been encouraged throughout the entire process to participate. The disc is a culmination, not a beginning.

Of course, there will be issues raised and objections made in Rome—let them be. *But let them be in writing.* Let them withstand the same standard of reflection that every single word in the document will have undergone. When it comes to our Five Freedoms, unexplained political moves cannot undo what reasoned, thoughtful analysis has done. For this reason, reservations by countries considering the treaty in Rome must not be permitted. A reservation is when a government says that it will sign a treaty, but only part of it will be applied, or it will not be enforceable in court even though it has been signed. Reservations would make a mockery of all the focusing, thinking, and writing on the disc. There will be room for some changes to the document, as long as those changes are *written out and explained* for all to see. There is no room, however, for reservations.

Every word of the International Convention is designed to be enforceable in court. Part of the great success of the document in the decades, even centuries, ahead, is that it will gradually evolve through interpretation by judges, just as the European Convention continues to evolve today.[116] This legal evolution cannot function if countries can pick and choose, or disregard, legal interpretations. All people in all countries are entitled to the same Five Freedoms—their application cannot be limited by government officials so that some people have them and some do not.

Let us be clear, however, that while reservations will not be permitted, this does not mean that an International Convention will be the only source of human rights law for all countries. To the contrary, every country is always free in its own domestic law to provide for protections for its citizens that are even greater than the protections in the International Convention. The Convention establishes only a minimum standard. The starting point for legal analysis in every case is always the law of the country in which the case arose. If the law in that country already protects the right at issue, then there is no need for the court even to consider the International Convention. Countries can expand rights if they so choose.

What countries, and the leaders who run them, cannot do is to carve out a niche whereby they place themselves above all others and say that the rule of law embodied in the Convention does not apply to them. Humanity's agreement to live together works because everyone is deemed equal, individuals and nations, and no one is "above the law." We will never have peace enforced by one brute person, or one brute nation, no matter how benevolent the individual or nation may be. Therefore, when we come to the table to decide together in Rome, we do so as equals, both as individuals and as nations, without reservations.

Our New Document

When we leave the table in Rome with an International Convention in hand, the Five Freedoms will finally be fully realized through the rule of law. The chains that have bound us to war and poverty will be broken. As Confucius counseled and Franklin Roosevelt envisioned, we *will* have looked ahead to find happiness rather than sorrow at hand. We *will* have gone upstream and, on finding a fence under construction, we will have rolled up our sleeves to complete it.[117]

CONCLUSION

Forward Together

2048 follows in the footsteps of John Humphrey, the principal drafter of the Universal Declartion of Human Rights

When you think back over this book, including the photographs of great leaders at the beginning of the chapters, it is clear that over the past sixty years a lot of progress has been made toward humanity reaching an agreement to live together. 2048 builds on this progress with a plan that will carry us through this 100-year turning point, so that we live in peace and prosperity, rather than war and want, by the year 2048.

It is fitting that the final image is of John Humphrey, a Canadian professor who became the Director of the United Nations Human Rights Division. As the Director, he lead the research and writing of the Universal Declaration of Human Rights. 2048 follows in his footsteps, along with those of many others you have read about in this book.

There is strength following in the footsteps of something hopeful, something worthwhile, both in our own lives and for future generations. Of course, it's not easy to construct a fence, and that's part of the reason so many people resort to ambulances, but it's time. New Internet technologies afford us the opportunity to reach an international agreement. In addition, the urgency of the situation with our environment at risk and trillions of dollars being wasted on preparation for war make this a time to act.

2048 can succeed, but it rests on each of us to contribute, even in a small way by becoming a member, through making a comment on the website, mentioning this book to someone, or anything else that brings a spark of awareness. It's satisfying to accomplish something with others, and while a movement such as 2048 may take time, the result is *enduring.*[118] 2048 is part of the natural evolution of humanity. Despite what some may say, we want to live together as a human family, and now we have the means to do so.

I thank you for your participation, and look forward to hearing from you. As I said at the beginning of the book, if you write to me, I will surely write you back.

RESOURCES

A: Universal Declaration of Human Rights

PREAMBLE

Whereas recognition of the inherent dignity and of the equal and inalienable rights of all members of the human family is the foundation of freedom, justice and peace in the world,

Whereas disregard and contempt for human rights have resulted in barbarous acts which have outraged the conscience of mankind, and the advent of a world in which human beings shall enjoy freedom of speech and belief and freedom from fear and want has been proclaimed as the highest aspiration of the common people,

Whereas it is essential, if man is not to be compelled to have recourse, as a last resort, to rebellion against tyranny and oppression, that human rights should be protected by the rule of law,

Whereas it is essential to promote the development of friendly relations between nations,

Whereas the peoples of the United Nations have in the Charter reaffirmed their faith in fundamental human rights, in the dignity and worth of the human person and in the equal rights of men and women and have determined to promote social progress and better standards of life in larger freedom,

Whereas Member States have pledged themselves to achieve, in cooperation with the United Nations, the promotion of universal respect for and observance of human rights and fundamental freedoms,

Whereas a common understanding of these rights and freedoms is of the greatest importance for the full realization of this pledge,

Now, Therefore THE GENERAL ASSEMBLY proclaims THIS UNIVERSAL DECLARATION OF HUMAN RIGHTS as a common standard of achievement for all peoples and all nations, to the end that every individual and every organ of society, keeping this Declaration constantly in mind, shall strive by teaching and education to promote respect for these rights and freedoms and by progressive measures, national and international, to secure their universal and effective recognition and observance, both among the peoples of Member States themselves and among the peoples of territories under their jurisdiction.

ARTICLE 1

All human beings are born free and equal in dignity and rights. They are endowed with reason and conscience and should act towards one another in a spirit of brotherhood.

ARTICLE 2

Everyone is entitled to all the rights and freedoms set forth in this Declaration, without distinction of any kind, such as race, colour, sex, language, religion, political or other opinion, national or social origin, property, birth or other status. Furthermore, no distinction shall be made on the basis of the political, jurisdictional or international status of the country or territory to which a person belongs, whether it be independent, trust, non-self-governing or under any other limitation of sovereignty.

ARTICLE 3

Everyone has the right to life, liberty and security of person.

ARTICLE 4

No one shall be held in slavery or servitude; slavery and the slave trade shall be prohibited in all their forms.

ARTICLE 5

No one shall be subjected to torture or to cruel, inhuman or degrading treatment or punishment.

ARTICLE 6

Everyone has the right to recognition everywhere as a person before the law.

ARTICLE 7

All are equal before the law and are entitled without any discrimination to equal protection of the law. All are entitled to equal protection against any discrimination in violation of this Declaration and against any incitement to such discrimination.

ARTICLE 8

Everyone has the right to an effective remedy by the competent national tribunals for acts violating the fundamental rights granted him by the constitution or by law.

ARTICLE 9

No one shall be subjected to arbitrary arrest, detention or exile.

ARTICLE 10

Everyone is entitled in full equality to a fair and public hearing by an independent and impartial tribunal, in the determination of his rights and obligations and of any criminal charge against him.

ARTICLE 11

1. Everyone charged with a penal offence has the right to be presumed innocent until proved guilty according to law in a public trial at which he has had all the guarantees necessary for his defence.
2. No one shall be held guilty of any penal offence on account of any act or omission which did not constitute a penal offence, under national or international law, at the time when it was committed. Nor shall a heavier penalty be imposed than the one that was applicable at the time the penal offence was committed.

ARTICLE 12

No one shall be subjected to arbitrary interference with his privacy, family, home or correspondence, nor to attacks on his honour and reputation. Everyone has the right to the protection of the law against such interference or attacks.

ARTICLE 13

1. Everyone has the right to freedom of movement and residence within the borders of each state.

2. Everyone has the right to leave any country, including his own, and to return to his country.

ARTICLE 14

1. Everyone has the right to seek and to enjoy in other countries asylum from persecution.
2. This right may not be invoked in the case of prosecutions genuinely arising from nonpolitical crimes or from acts contrary to the purposes and principles of the United Nations.

ARTICLE 15

1. Everyone has the right to a nationality.
2. No one shall be arbitrarily deprived of his nationality nor denied the right to change his nationality.

ARTICLE 16

1. Men and women of full age, without any limitation due to race, nationality or religion, have the right to marry and to found a family. They are entitled to equal rights as to marriage, during marriage and at its dissolution.
2. Marriage shall be entered into only with the free and full consent of the intending spouses.
3. The family is the natural and fundamental group unit of society and is entitled to protection by society and the State.

ARTICLE 17

1. Everyone has the right to own property alone as well as in association with others.
2. No one shall be arbitrarily deprived of his property.

ARTICLE 18

Everyone has the right to freedom of thought, conscience and religion; this right includes freedom to change his religion or belief, and freedom, either alone or in community with others and in public or private, to manifest his religion or belief in teaching, practice, worship and observance.

ARTICLE 19

Everyone has the right to freedom of opinion and expression; this right includes freedom to hold opinions without interference and to seek, receive and impart information and ideas through any media and regardless of frontiers.

ARTICLE 20

1. Everyone has the right to freedom of peaceful assembly and association.
2. No one may be compelled to belong to an association.

ARTICLE 21

1. Everyone has the right to take part in the government of his country, directly or through freely chosen representatives.
2. Everyone has the right of equal access to public service in his country.
3. The will of the people shall be the basis of the authority of government; this will shall be expressed in periodic and genuine elections which shall be by universal and equal suffrage and shall be held by secret vote or by equivalent free voting procedures.

ARTICLE 22

Everyone, as a member of society, has the right to social security and is entitled to realization, through national effort and international cooperation and in accordance with the organization and resources of each State, of the economic, social and cultural rights indispensable for his dignity and the free development of his personality.

ARTICLE 23

1. Everyone has the right to work, to free choice of employment, to just and favourable conditions of work and to protection against unemployment.

2. Everyone, without any discrimination, has the right to equal pay for equal work.
3. Everyone who works has the right to just and favourable remuneration ensuring for himself and his family an existence worthy of human dignity, and supplemented, if necessary, by other means of social protection.
4. Everyone has the right to form and to join trade unions for the protection of his interests.

ARTICLE 24

Everyone has the right to rest and leisure, including reasonable limitation of working hours and periodic holidays with pay.

ARTICLE 25

1. Everyone has the right to a standard of living adequate for the health and well-being of himself and of his family, including food, clothing, housing and medical care and necessary social services, and the right to security in the event of unemployment, sickness, disability, widowhood, old age or other lack of livelihood in circumstances beyond his control.
2. Motherhood and childhood are entitled to special care and assistance. All children, whether born in or out of wedlock, shall enjoy the same social protection.

ARTICLE 26

1. Everyone has the right to education. Education shall be free, at least in the elementary and fundamental stages. Elementary education shall be compulsory. Technical and professional education shall be made generally available and higher education shall be equally accessible to all on the basis of merit.
2. Education shall be directed to the full development of the human personality and to the strengthening of respect for human rights and fundamental freedoms. It shall promote understanding, tolerance and friendship among all nations, racial or religious groups, and shall further the activities of the United Nations for the maintenance of peace.
3. Parents have a prior right to choose the kind of education that shall be given to their children.

ARTICLE 27

1. Everyone has the right freely to participate in the cultural life of the community, to enjoy the arts and to share in scientific advancement and its benefits.
2. Everyone has the right to the protection of the moral and material interests resulting from any scientific, literary or artistic production of which he is the author.

ARTICLE 28

Everyone is entitled to a social and international order in which the rights and freedoms set forth in this Declaration can be fully realized.

ARTICLE 29

1. Everyone has duties to the community in which alone the free and full development of his personality is possible.
2. In the exercise of his rights and freedoms, everyone shall be subject only to such limitations as are determined by law solely for the purpose of securing due recognition and respect for the rights and freedoms of others and of meeting the just requirements of morality, public order and the general welfare in a democratic society.
3. These rights and freedoms may in no case be exercised contrary to the purposes and principles of the United Nations.

ARTICLE 30

Nothing in this Declaration may be interpreted as implying for any State, group or person any right to engage in any activity or to perform any act aimed at the destruction of any of the rights and freedoms set forth herein.

B: Draft International Convention on Human Rights, January 1, 2010

PREAMBLE

The States Parties to this Statute,

Considering the Universal Declaration of Human Rights proclaimed by the General Assembly of the United Nations on 10 December 1948;

Considering that all peoples are united by common bonds, their cultures pieced together in a shared heritage, including numerous religious beliefs;

Considering that the people are entitled to put their social contract with each other and those in government in writing to ensure fundamental human rights as part of their social order;

Considering that the Universal Declaration aims at securing the universal and effective recognition and observance of the Rights therein declared, and that many of the Rights declared in the Universal Declaration remain unrealized and unenforceable for billions of children, women and men in our international community;

Whereas disregard and contempt for human rights have resulted in barbarous acts which have outraged the conscience of mankind, and the advent of a world in which human beings shall enjoy freedom of speech and belief and freedom from want and fear has been proclaimed as the highest aspiration of the common people;

Whereas it is essential, if man is not to be compelled to have recourse, as a last resort, to rebellion against tyranny and oppression, that human rights should be protected by the rule of law;

Reaffirming that it is the duty of every State that is a signatory to the Universal Declaration, in accordance with Article 28 of that Declaration, to create a social and international order in which the rights and freedoms set forth in the Declaration can be fully realized;

Recognizing that the European Convention on Human Rights, the Inter-American Convention on Human Rights, and the African Convention on Human Rights have taken valuable first steps in making rights in the Universal Declaration enforceable in domestic courts of law and in regional courts enforcing those Conventions;

Deciding that these first steps be followed by others, including the expansion of regional courts and the creation of an International Convention on Human Rights with an International Court of Human Rights to enforce it;

Deciding that the International Court of Human Rights established under this Statute is intended to be an International Civil Court complementary to the International Criminal Court and to national courts, and that national domestic courts may interpret their own Constitutions to provide greater protections for human rights than those in the International Convention;

Being resolved, to achieve the full realization of international human rights today and for future generations, and to provide for the legal enforcement of the rights stated in the Universal Declaration, as well as for environmental rights that are not in the Declaration, but are recognized today as equally important;

Have agreed as follows:

ARTICLE 1 (OBLIGATION TO RESPECT HUMAN RIGHTS)

The High Contracting Parties shall secure to everyone within their jurisdiction the fundamental rights, and a legal process to enforce them, defined in this Convention. Every man, woman and child is a person before the law, and these rights apply whether they are in their homeland or any foreign land.

Section I: Fundamental Rights

ARTICLE 2 (FREE SPEECH)

1. Everyone has the right to freedom of opinion and expression; this right includes freedom to hold opinions without interference and to see, receive and impart information and ideas through any media and regardless of borders. No one may be coerced into expressing his or her views and convictions or into renouncing them. The only exception is that the urging of physical violence against individuals or groups based on race, reli-

gion, gender, or sexual orientation, is impermissible.

2. Written documents and other forms of information may be distributed within the distance of an outstretched arm from one person to another. This right to hand out information shall apply to any public place as well as private property where the public has been openly invited such as a shopping center or marketplace.
3. The freedom of the mass media shall be guaranteed. The dissemination of information, including broadcasts, may not be preempted without a court order finding that the information presents a serious threat to national security and an immediate serious danger to the lives of citizens, or that the information urges physical violence against individuals or groups based on race, religion, gender or sexual orientation.

ARTICLE 3 (FREEDOM OF ASSOCIATION)

Everyone shall have the right to freedom of association, including the right, in small groups or large ones, to gather peacefully, without weapons, and to hold meetings, rallies, demonstrations, marches and pickets. This right shall apply to government property open to the public, even if the property is only temporarily open for a public event, and to private property where the public has been openly invited such as a shopping center or marketplace.

ARTICLE 4 (PETITION)

Everyone shall have the right to submit petitions in writing to government authorities without punishment or retribution.

ARTICLE 5 (FREEDOM OF RELIGION)

Everyone has the right of freedom of religion and to choose his or her own religious beliefs. No person may be prosecuted or discriminated against simply for holding a certain belief. The government shall not use public taxes to fund any religious activities or organizations, but religious organizations shall not be taxed. No governmental organization shall establish a particular religion.

ARTICLE 6 (EQUALITY)

Everyone is equal before the law. Men and women have equal rights and share the right to human dignity. Women have an equal right to the same wage for the same work as men. Everyone is entitled to equal protection under law, and nobody shall be prejudiced or favored because of his or her birth, race, sex, sexual orientation, marital status, pregnancy, age, color, disability, wealth, language, national origin, faith, religion or political opinion. To promote the achievement of equality, legislative and other measures designed to protect or advance persons or categories of persons, disadvantaged by past unfair discrimination may be taken.

ARTICLE 7 (REPRESENTATION)

1. All power to govern emanates from the people through their choice of representatives and not from military position, religion, caste, heredity or any nonelective title or position. Every citizen may seek elective office and nonincumbent candidates must be given a fair opportunity to compete with those who are presently in office. No elected representative shall serve more than twelve consecutive years in the same position. Only individuals, not corporations or other entities, shall be allowed to contribute money or other assets to candidates or ballot measures, but individuals may combine to contribute as a group. The total annual contribution by any individual, whether it is to one candidate or divided among several candidates and ballot measures, shall not exceed 30 percent of the median income for the country in which the person resides.
2. Candidates for national or state legislative or executive positions shall be given adequate free time on television and other media to promote a well informed electorate and reduce the need for candidates to raise large amounts of money to communicate with voters. A minimum of 30 hours of free national broadcast time and 20 hours of

State broadcast time, during times of large viewing audiences, shall be reserved for the 100 day period prior to the election. The allocation of such time shall be defined by law, but shall include any candidate able to show support of 5 percent or greater of the general population.

ARTICLE 8 (VOTING)

1. Everyone, regardless of sex, race, religion or any other classification, is entitled to a representative form of government. All people eighteen years or older shall have the right to vote in a secret ballot for their representatives. Each vote shall be given equal weight and each voter shall be able to vote directly for any representative who represents them. No tax may be placed on the right to vote, nor shall any test or property be required to be eligible to vote. Voting shall be made easily accessible to all, including the ability to vote by mail, or other methods. Workers have the right to leave work to vote in State-wide or national elections without a reduction in pay.
2. Registration to vote shall be mandatory for anyone 18 years or older. No citizen who has legally resided in one place within a country for 30 days shall be denied the right to vote at that location. Everyone has the responsibility to participate in the governance of his or her society and, at a minimum, to cast a ballot during elections for statewide and national office. Repeated failure to

cast a ballot may result in the loss of privileges. The ballot submitted may be blank or partially completed.

ARTICLE 9 (ENVIRONMENT)

Everyone has the right to a clean and healthy environment, including water that is safe to drink and air that is safe to breathe, as defined by law. There is also a right to the preservation of species and their habitat, both for the benefit of future generations and for the species themselves. Major activities undertaken by either the government or a private person or company that have significant environmental impacts must allow for public participation in the review and permit process.

ARTICLE 10 (EDUCATION)

1. Everyone shall have the right to education. Access to preschool, if desired, shall be guaranteed and free from age three. Primary and secondary education in public educational institutions shall be guaranteed and free. Parents have the responsibility to enroll their children in school, unless comparable schooling is offered at home, as defined by law. Students must attend school, or be home schooled, through a secondary degree.
2. Everyone shall have the right to receive, on a competitive basis for entrance to schools, at least four years of higher education, free of charge or

at a low fee, as defined by law. For those who elect not to attend four years of higher education, and prefer vocational training in a specific field, that too shall be provided according to his or her individual abilities and the number of positions available, as defined by law. Everyone shall also have an equal opportunity to receive graduate education according to his or her individual abilities and the number of positions available, as defined by law. Graduate education shall be free of charge or a reasonable fee. Everyone who receives free or low cost education and/or graduate school education has a responsibility to work temporarily on behalf of society, as defined by law.

ARTICLE 11 (HEALTH CARE)

Everyone has a right to free or low cost health care, including vision, dental and mental care, as defined by law. Health care includes the right to sufficient food necessary for good health, along with information on nutrition, sexual education, prenatal and pediatric care, as well as curative and rehabilitative medical care, all as defined by law.

ARTICLE 12 (SHELTER)

Everyone has the right, along with his or her family, to shelter with safe water, electricity, and sanitary conditions, as defined by law. Every person or family given assistance with shelter has a responsibility to temporarily work on behalf of society, as defined by law.

ARTICLE 13 (PROPERTY)

Everyone has the right to own, buy and sell property. No one may be deprived of his or her property without due process. The government may not take private property, except for public use. Just compensation must be paid to any person, association, or company with a legal interest in the property before it is taken. Just compensation shall be determined by a jury of lay people in the community where the property is located.

ARTICLE 14 (LABOR)

Everyone has the right to choose his or her occupation or profession and place of work. Everyone also has the right to form and join a union and to participate in the activities and programs of a trade union, including the right to strike and collective bargaining. The right to strike may be limited only in a national emergency and then, only temporarily. Everyone is entitled to a living minimum wage and to financial assistance in the case of old age or the inability to work, as defined by law. Everyone receiving financial assistance also has the responsibility to work to the best of his or her physical and mental abilities, as defined by law.

ARTICLE 15 (FAIR PROCEDURES)

Everyone is entitled to fair procedures to safeguard his or her rights. No one may be deprived of life, liberty, or property without due process of law. Administrative and judicial actions must be lawful and procedurally fair. Everyone whose rights have been adversely affected by administrative or judicial action has the right to be given written reasons, including the applicable law relied on by the decision maker. All judicial appellate rulings shall be published in writing and placed on the Internet so that they are freely available to all.

ARTICLE 16 (INDEPENDENT JUDICIARY)

In addition to the people themselves, judges are the guardians of these rights. Judges must be independent and impartial at all times. No person shall give nor shall any judge receive any money, gift or service other than the judge's official salary. No party to a case, nor any person acting on their behalf, may speak to a judge about a case without the presence of, or at least knowledge of, the other party. Politicians, their agents, or other third parties also may not discuss with a judge any pending matter. Any judge found to have improperly received money, gifts or services shall lose his or her judicial position, return to the public treasury that which was wrongly accepted and serve time in jail, as defined by law. Judicial independence requires financial independence and no judge shall earn less than three times the national median income.

ARTICLE 17 (FUNDING)

Recognizing that the rule of law and rights herein benefit the citizens and businesses of all countries, each country shall annually contribute one percent of its gross national product into an international fund for the use and support of educational, healthcare and judicial facilities and salaries internationally, including the Courts described in articles 33–40. The funding shall be distributed by an international non-governmental organization composed of leaders appointed in a similar manner to the judges on the International Court. These leaders from many professions and backgrounds shall be dedicated to the fulfillment of the rights herein, and, like judges, independent of the governments that appointed them.

ARTICLE 18 (SEARCH AND SEIZURE)

Everyone is protected from unreasonable searches and seizures of their person, home and belongings. Searches and seizures must be authorized by a court based on written documents, including reasons and evidence, submitted before the search or seizure is approved.

ARTICLE 19 (ARREST)

1. No person shall be arrested or imprisoned without a judicial warrant that is based on written documents submitted before the warrant is approved. Such warrant must state reasons for the arrest, including a reference to the law alleged violated, and must be served on the arrestee at the moment of arrest unless a person is arrested during or shortly after the commission of a crime and there is evidence linking them to the crime. Everyone shall be informed at the time of the arrest or detention of the right to consult a lawyer without delay and to remain silent until they have spoken with a lawyer. An opportunity must be provided within six hours of arrest to communicate by telephone, or in person, with an attorney and a family member or friend. An arrestee also has the right to use adequate facilities to prepare a defense. If the arrestee lacks funds for an attorney, then the government must provide one.
2. Everyone shall have the right to be publicly charged in a courtroom open to the public, including the news media, and to have the validity of the arrest or detention determined within 72 hours by an independent judge. He or she shall be released if the arrest or detention is not lawful. If the defendant insists, trial shall commence not more than 6 months from the date of arrest.

Provided that a defendant can show that there is no genuine risk that he or she will not appear at trial, the defendant shall be released pending trial unless it can be shown that they are a danger to others.

ARTICLE 20 (FAIR TRIAL)

1. Everyone who is charged with any criminal offense has the right to a fair public hearing by an independent and impartial court and counsel to represent them. Everyone charged has the right to be presumed innocent until proven guilty according to law and everyone shall have the right to a trial by jury of not less than six of his or her fellow citizens when the penalty for the offense could be imprisonment for more than 3 months. A jury decision to convict shall be unanimous.
2. Everyone accused of a crime has the right not to be compelled to be a witness or to confess guilt as well as the right to be present at the trial, to be heard, and to present a defense including the right to examine the witnesses for the prosecution and to obtain the attendance and examination of witnesses for the defense under the same conditions as the prosecution.
3. Everyone accused of a crime shall have the right to have the free assistance of an interpreter if he or she cannot understand or speak the language used in court. No one shall be convicted of any offense for any act or omission which did

not constitute an offense under the law at the time it occurred. If convicted of an offense, everyone has the right to appeal to a higher court. No one who has been finally acquitted, convicted of, or pardoned for an offense shall be tried or punished for it again; nor may punishment be more severe than punishment in force at the time the crime was committed.

ARTICLE 21 (LIFE, PERSONAL FREEDOM, SECURITY)

Everyone has the right to life, personal freedom, and security. Slavery or indentured servitude is abolished. Torture, cruel and unusual punishment and the death penalty are all prohibited. Further, for security from widespread annihilation, the use of nuclear weapons is prohibited. The creation or use of chemical or biological weapons is forbidden.

ARTICLE 22 (CULTURE)

Everyone has a right to his or her cultural identity, including the right to use his or her own language and engage in his or her own cultural traditions, provided they do not prejudice the traditions of others, or violate the rights embodied in this Convention. The government, however, may require schooling in particular languages and broad study of cultural history.

ARTICLE 23 (CITIZENSHIP)

No citizen may have their citizenship revoked. Citizens have the responsibility to share in the burden of public expenditures including the responsibility to pay taxes, as defined by law. Every citizen of a country has the right to freedom of movement and residence within that country and the right to enter freely and leave his or her country of citizenship.

ARTICLE 24 (MARRIAGE)

People of full age have the right to marry and to found a family. Men and women are entitled to equal rights at marriage, during marriage and at its dissolution. Marriage shall be entered into only with the free and full consent of the intending spouses.

ARTICLE 25 (CHILDREN)

1) Every child has the right to a name and a nationality from birth and to parental care, or to appropriate alternative care when removed from the family environment. Children 16 or younger shall not work during school hours unless provisions for home schooling have been established, as defined by law. Parents shall have responsibility for raising and caring for their children and must assure that, in partnership

with the government, their children complete school through a secondary degree.

2. If a child is detained, then he or she has the right to be kept separately from detained persons over the age of 18 years and kept in conditions that take account of the child's age. No child under 18 may be used in armed conflict, even voluntarily.

ARTICLE 26 (MEDICAL DECISIONS)

Everyone has the right to bodily and psychological integrity, which includes the right to access contraception and the right to make decisions concerning reproduction. Everyone also has the right of control over his or her body, including the authority to end life-extending treatment. No one may be subjected to medical or scientific experiments without his or her informed consent.

ARTICLE 27 (PRIVACY)

Everyone shall have the right to privacy in his or her home, hotel room, vehicle, or vessel and to have interpersonal relations as they choose. This right includes all communications between people, in public or private that they intend to keep confidential. Eavesdropping is forbidden without a court order as part of a criminal investigation. Such order shall only be issued on evidence submitted in writing to the judge issuing the order.

ARTICLE 28 (INFORMATION)

Everyone has a right to access, obtain, and correct information collected about them by the government, or by any private individual or company for a commercial purpose, unless such information is part of a criminal investigation or prosecution.

ARTICLE 29 (INTELLECTUAL PROPERTY)

Everyone has the right to engage in cultural, artistic and scientific fields and to the profits of their work. Authors have exclusive international rights to use, publish or reproduce their works. Patents and copyrights are protected and recognized by all people and all nations. Any person or company whose work is misused is entitled to damages.

ARTICLE 30 (HABEAS CORPUS)

Everyone in custody has the right to a public hearing before a court if he or she makes a claim of being held in violation of this Convention, even if he or she has been convicted pursuant to court processes. All possibilities for appeal within the country in which the person is held must be exhausted before this right can be exercised. Exceptions for immediate review by regional courts and the international court may be made on a strong and convincing showing that redress from the domestic court is untimely or impracticable.

ARTICLE 31 (RESPONSIBILITY FOR VIOLATION OF RIGHTS)

Any private individual, private or public company, or public official, agent or employee of the government, who violates the rights set forth in this Convention is not immune from liability, qualified or otherwise, and is responsible to pay damages, including attorneys, fees and costs, to the person whose rights have been violated. All government bodies are liable under civil law for actions or omissions made by government officials, agents or employees in the exercise of their functions which result in violations of the rights set forth herein.

ARTICLE 32 (TRIAL FOR VIOLATION OF RIGHTS)

Any person, organization, or company who claims a violation of this Convention by government officials, agents, or employees or any private individual or private or public company shall have a right to trial by a jury of at least six of his or her fellow citizens. The jury shall decide liability and damages and need not be unanimous.

Section II: International Court of Human Rights

ARTICLE 33 (COMPOSITION OF THE COURT)

An International Court of Human Rights shall be created. The Court shall be composed of one judge from each country that has ratified this Convention in its entirety, without reservation, and agreed that it is enforceable as part of domestic law. Regional courts, subject to review by the International Court, and composed of one judge from each country in the region, shall also be organized through the continued operation of existing regional courts, or the creation of new ones.

ARTICLE 34 (TERMS OF SERVICE FOR JUSTICES)

The judges' terms for the International Court of Human Rights and the regional courts shall be 6 years, with terms to be staggered, as feasible. No judge may serve more than two terms. Should staggering result in appointments of two years or less, then the judge shall be allowed an additional term. Judges shall consider claims brought under this International Convention based on the sanctity of the right and independently from the personal and political pressures of the country that nominated them. The nomination of judges shall be made by the country which they are from and approved by an absolute majority vote of the countries that have ratified this Convention.

ARTICLE 35 (APPLICATION IN ALL COUNTRIES)

The rights included in this Convention may be raised before the courts of all countries. The courts in each country with jurisdiction to consider claims brought under the Constitution of that country shall also consider claims brought under this Convention. These rights also apply and may be raised in all regional courts.

ARTICLE 36 (SUPREMACY OF RIGHTS)

This Convention establishes a minimum standard to which all people are entitled. These rights are superior to any law that conflicts with them. The Courts of all countries shall uphold the Convention and shall declare as illegal any law, other legal act, or procedure that violates the rights stated herein. Any country may enact a law or interpret its own Constitution to provide for rights greater than those guaranteed by this Convention.

ARTICLE 37 (CLAIMS FIRST BROUGHT IN COUNTRY OF ORIGIN)

Cases shall be brought through the established domestic court system for the country where the claim arose. Any person shall have standing to bring a claim for violation of this Convention if they allege that there has been a violation of a right or rights, and that they have been affected, either directly or indirectly, by the violation. No claim of a violation may be brought before the International Court of Human Rights until the claim has first been brought in the domestic courts of the country in which the claim arose. Appeal must be made to the highest domestic appellate court, as well as any regional court, before review will be made by the International Court of Human Rights. Exceptions may be made on a showing of strong and convincing evidence that redress from the domestic court is untimely or impracticable, and then the case may originate in the regional court.

ARTICLE 38 (COURT HEARINGS)

The location of the International Court of Human Rights shall be selected by a majority of the parties to this Convention. The Court shall have an annual calendar with all cases decided by written opinion within the same annual session in which they are considered. The location of the Court shall be selected, and the hearing of cases shall commence, after 45 countries have ratified this Convention.

Cases are accepted for hearing by a vote of one third of the sitting judges at the time of the vote. The Court may appoint a review committee of less than one third for initial consideration of cases, however, a third of judges may bypass this committee, and a third of the judges must agree to the recommendation of the review committee for a hearing to take place. The vote to accept a case is made in private, but judges are free to publicly explain their position for or against accepting a case, and may write an opinion so stating to be published by the Court.

Cases are heard by Chambers of fifteen judges, fourteen randomly selected, along with the judge from the country in which the case arose. A Chamber's decision may be reviewed by two thirds of the Court, randomly selected, along with the judge from the country in which the case arose, if a majority of the judges on the Court agree to review it. Hearings shall take place at the International Court unless a majority of the judges of the Court decide that a hearing is appropriate elsewhere.

ARTICLE 39 (COURT DECISIONS)

The International Court of Human Rights shall set its own procedures for the consideration of cases. Once a case has been selected, oral argument shall be the norm and a written decision by the majority of the Chamber, or the majority on appeal from a

Chamber, shall be published in an official report. Dissenting opinions shall also be published and each judge may write separately or join in an opinion by a group. All judges shall be assisted by at least four law clerks, selected by the judge, three of whom shall be from countries other than the judge's home country.

ARTICLE 40 (ENFORCEMENT OF DECISIONS)

Decisions of the International Court of Human Rights are enforceable through the domestic courts from which the case arose. Failure to comply with the decisions of the Court may result in expulsion from the Convention and the Court on a vote of two thirds of the judges of the Court.

NOTES

[1] This phrase was found in a fortune cookie by the author, but others have expressed a similar sentiment. The Buddha taught that the bonds of human beings are self-applied. "Each man his own prison makes." Raghavan Iyer, *Parapolitics: Toward the City of Man* (Oxford: Oxford University Press, 1979), p.225. Rousseau began his famous work, *Social Contract,* by stating, "Man is born free, and everywhere he is in chains." Geoffrey Cumberlege, *Social Contract: Essays by Locke, Hume and Rousseau* (London: Oxford University Press, 1953). Jean-Jacques Rousseau, *Contract Social* (1762), p.240.

[2] Some human rights scholars will be aghast at this new use of an "International Bill of Rights." They will say it is an affront to the existing International Bill of Rights that is composed of the Universal Declaration of Human Rights and the twin Covenants on Economic, Social, and Cultural Rights and Civil and Political Rights. I have two responses: (1) How many courts actually enforce the Universal Declaration and the twin Covenants? Very few. (2) I use the term "Bill of Rights" restrictively, to include judicial review and enforcement by courts. Even when there is some enforcement of the Covenants, this enforcement is limited to state reports or, if the optional protocols have been agreed to, valuable but unenforceable opinions by Committees. While

the Universal Declaration and the Covenants represent the emergence of an International Bill of Rights, and are a great accomplishment, they do not constitute one. It's time to admit this fact. Repeatedly calling these three pieces an International Bill of Rights will not make it so.

[3] George Orwell, *Animal Farm* (New York: Signet, 1946), p.83. (Pigs slaughter the other animals.)

[4] Akbar Ganji, *The Road to Democracy in Iran* (Cambridge, MA: Boston Review, 2008), pp.25–26. ("Our movement advocates reformist change rather than revolution. It does not foment rebellion, nor does it support military action from inside or outside the country. We do not believe that historic change occurs in leaps.")

[5] Paul Hawken, *Blessed Unrest: How the Largest Movement in the World Came into Being and Why No One Saw It Coming* (New York: Viking, 2007), p.191. ("There may be as many as 10 million nonprofits in the world.")

[6] Einstein, The Brainy Quote, www.brainyquote.com.

[7] John P. Kaminski, *The Quotable Jefferson* (Princeton, NJ: Princeton University Press, 2006), p.18.

[8] James Forman, *That Mad Game: War and the Chances for Peace* (New York: Scribner, 2006), p.143.

[9] www.ipcc.ch. The Intergovernmental Panel on Climate Change is a good example of worldwide collaborative research that can be accomplished through the Internet. Thousands of scientists all over the world contribute to the work of the IPCC on a voluntary basis as authors, contributors, and reviewers. The IPCC was honored with the Nobel Peace Prize in 2007. We should use a similar approach to research and draft an International Bill of Rights that is enforceable in all countries.

[10] There is a shortage of teaching resources regarding the Universal Declaration of Human Rights, even though, for example, the California Education Code requires that the evolution of human rights be taught. See Education Code Section 51226.3; *Model Curriculum for Human Rights and Genocide* (2000). "By studying the United Nations' Universal Declaration of Human Rights, students should learn that concern for human rights is not confined to Western nations; it is an international issue." Nonetheless, when I ask my UC Berkeley students on the first day of class how many of them learned about the Universal Decla-

ration in high school, out of a class of sixty or seventy only three or four will raise their hand. It is my hope that 2048 will be used in high schools.

[11] Chester Bowles, *Promises to Keep: My Years in Public Life, 1941–1969* (New York: HarperCollins, 1971), p.451.

[12] Elie Wiesel, *Night* (New York: Hill & Wang, 1960), p.13.

[13] Johannes Morsink, *The Universal Declaration of Human Rights: Origins, Drafting, and Intent* (Philadelphia: University of Pennsylvania Press, 1999), p.43. (The Universal Declaration was intended to counter "Nazification.")

[14] Jim continues to practice with Morrison and Foerster and he serves on the board of the 2048 Project.

[15] Franklin Delano Roosevelt, "The Four Freedoms," *American Rhetoric* (January 6, 1941): http://www.americanrhetoric.com/speeches/fdrthefourfreedoms.htm.

[16] John P. Humphrey, *Human Rights and the United Nations: A Great Adventure* (New York: Transnational Publishers, 1984), p.12. (World War II, unlike any previous war, was a war to vindicate human rights.)

[17] Paul Gordon Lauren, *The Evolution of International Human Rights, Visions Seen* (Philadelphia: University of Pennsylvania Press, 1998), pp.189–190; William Korey, *NGOs and the*

Universal Declaration of Human Rights: A Curious Grapevine (New York: Palgrave, 1998), pp.38–39.

[18] Harry Truman, *Truman Speaks,* Cyril Clemens, ed. (New York: Kraus Reprint, 1969), p.56.

[19] Concerns about the impact of enforceable human rights on segregation continued into the debate about the Covenants. During the drafting of the Covenants, the prospect of ratifying an international human rights document that outlawed racial discrimination aroused considerable opposition within the U.S. Senate. Southern Democrats in particular feared the Covenants would become a backdoor method for enacting civil rights legislation and could be used to invalidate Jim Crow laws in the South. This strong Senate opposition ultimately caused the Eisenhower administration to abandon its support for these international human rights treaties. See Kaufman, Natalie Hevener, and David Whiteman, "Opposition to Human Rights Treaties in the United States Senate: The Legacy of the Bricker Amendment," *Human Rights Quarterly* 10. no.3 (August 1988), pp.309–337; Christopher Roberts. "Exploring the Fractures within Human Rights: An Empirical Study of Resistance," PhD dissertation (Ann Arbor: University of Michigan, 2010).

[20] Kirsten Sellars, *The Rise and Rise of Human Rights* (Sparkford: Sutton, 2002), pp.18–20.

[21] The United States clearly stated its position that the Universal Declaration would *not* be an enforceable document; Eleanor Roosevelt told the General Assembly, "In giving our approval to the Declaration today, it is of primary importance that we keep clearly in mind the basic character of the document. It is not and does not purport to be a statement of law or legal obligation. It is a declaration of basic principles of human rights and freedoms, to be stamped with the approval of the General Assembly by a formal vote of its members, and to serve as a common standard of achievement for all peoples of all nations. *Bulletin of the State Department* 19(1948), p.751.

[22] H. Lauterpacht, *International Law and Human Rights* (New York: Praeger, 1950), p.420.

[23] The Charter of Fundamental Rights of the European Union: www.europarl.europa.eu/charter.

[24] See Walter Truett Anderson, *All Connected Now: Life in the First Global Civilization* (Boulder, CO: Westview Press, 2001), p.86. ("Progress into a world with universal war crimes laws and human rights guarantees obviously won't be either easy or peaceful. But it will happen.")

[25] Mary Ann Glendon, *A World Made New: Eleanor Roosevelt and the Universal Declaration of*

Human Rights (New York: Random House, 2001), p.170. ("'It was after midnight when I left the Palais de Chaillot,' she wrote. 'I was tired. I wondered whether a mere statement of rights, without legal obligation, would inspire governments to see that these rights were observed.'")

[26] Juliet Eilperin, "Gore Launches Ambitious Advocacy Campaign on Climate," *Washington Post,* March 31, 2008.

[27] Kaminski, *The Quotable Jefferson,* p.83.

[28] Starbucks coffee cup, "The Way I See It," #7.

[29] Yochai Benkler, *The Wealth of Networks: How Social Production Transforms Markets and Freedom* (New Haven: Yale University Press, 2006), p.375. (Benkler recognizes the sense of common purpose that is emerging through projects like 2048 because they "offer a type of relationship that is nonhierarchical and organized in a radically decentralized pattern. Their social valence is given by some combination of the shared experience of joint creativity they enable, as well as their efficacy—their ability to give their users a sense of common purpose and mutual support in achieving it.")

[30] See www.2048.edu, "resources."

[31] Paul Hawken, *Blessed Unrest: How the Largest Movement in the World Came into Being and Why No One Saw it Coming* (New York: Viking, 2007), p.191. ("There may be as many as 10

million nonprofits in the world.") See also www.wiserearth.org for information about many of these organizations.

[32] *The Chronicle of Philanthropy 21,* no.22, (October 1, 2009), p.31.

[33] Confucius, *The Analects* (500BCE), Section 3, Part 15, p.38.

[34] This story was told to the author by Caroline Avery, a member of the 2048 Project board and for several years the President of the Durfee Foundation.

[35] Foundation Center's Statistical Information Service. *Foundation Giving Adjusted for Inflation, 1975 to 2007.* In 2007, U.S. Foundations provided 44.3 billion: http://foundationcenter.org/findfunders/statistics/pdf/02_found_growth/2007/05_07.pdf]. See also European Foundation Center, *Foundations in the European Union: Facts and Figures: Report on the Work of the EFC Research Task Force,* p.8: "The 58,588 public-benefit foundations surveyed in 14 EU countries reported total spending of €46bn, an average of €1m per foundation. German public-benefit foundations show the highest total expenditure."

[36] The Whitman Institute, with its Executive Director, John Esterle, has been crucial to the 2048 effort to break a path upstream.

[37] President Franklin D. Roosevelt, Congressional Address, January 6, 1941: http://www.m

tholyoke.edu/acad/intrel/WorldWar2/fdr23.htm.

[38] Eleanor Roosevelt, *What I Hope to Leave Behind* (New York: Carlson, 1995), p.511.

[39] See Elizabeth Borgwardt, *A New Deal for the World: America's Vision for Human Rights,* (Cambridge: Belknap Press, 2007).

[40] *Atlantic Charter,* untitled telegram in Roosevelt's handwriting, "For Delivery to Press and Radio EST on Thursday, Aug 14," FDR Papers as President.

[41] Roger Highfield, "DNA Survey Finds All Humans Are 99.9% Same" *Telegraph,* December 20, 2002).

[42] This figure was compiled through the sum of 1% of each country: http://www.studentsoftheworld.info.

[43] Robert Scheer, *The Pornography of Power: Why Defense Spending Must Be Cut* (New York: Twelve, 2009), p.166. (combining both defense department and supplementary spending for the Iraq and Afghanistan war).

[44] Naomi Wolf, *Give Me Liberty* (New York: Simon & Schuster, 2008), p.4.

[45] Don Edward Fehrenbacher, *Lincoln's Speeches and Writings 1859–1865* (Des Moines, IA: Library of America, 1989), p.109.

[46] Lord Charnwood, *Abraham Lincoln* (New York: Holt, 1917), p.147.

[47] Frank K. Kelly, *Waging Peace II: What Humanity Can Do: The Power of Citizens* (Chicago: Noble Press, 1992), p.210.

[48] Still, I don't feel singled out or slighted. There have always been briars along the path less traveled. See Richard Falk, *Achieving Human Rights* (New York: Routledge, 2009), p.202. ("The Citizen Pilgrim combines a discontent with the world as s/he finds it with a dedication to an often demanding and generally solitary and hazardous journey to the future.")

[49] Cass R. Sunstein, *The Second Bill of Rights: FDR's Unfinished Revolution and Why We Need It More Than Ever* (New York: Basic Books, 2004), p.91.

[50] Sean Kay, *Global Security in the Twenty-First Century: The Quest for Power and the Search for Peace* (Lanham, MD: Rowman & Littlefield, 2006), p.280.

[51] For a perceptive observation of this trend, see Tom Ginsburg and Robert A. Kagan, ed., *Institutions and Public Law, Comparative Approaches* (New York: Lang, 2005), p.284. (Chapter 10, "Law, Courts, and Politics" by Martin Shapiro, "If these positive rights can not only be constitutionalized but placed within the realm of judicial review, then judges can not only intervene negatively to veto legislative and administrative cutbacks of entitlements but order legislative or administrative increases

in entitlement expenditure or even initiation of new entitlements.")

[52] Twenty-five hundred students drop out of U.S. high schools every day. November 1, 2009: http://abcnews.go.com.

[53] Joan Blades, *The Motherhood Manifesto* (New York: Nation, 2006), p.113 (Investing in after school education actually saves money because it cuts back on crime. Similar international savings can be realized.)

[54] For example, under the George W. Bush administration the 400 richest Americans came to have more wealth than the 150 million poorest Americans. Don Monkerud, July 4, 2009, "Consortium News," www.consortiumnews.com/2009/070409a.html. The consolidation of wealth is not only in America. "In Russia, following the collapse of USSR ... inequality there is dramatically higher than in any country in the West." Mark Buchanon, "The Mathematics of Inequality," *Australian Financial Review* (September 2002).

[55] "The developing world is poorer than we thought." World Bank, August 2008: http://www.globalissues.org/article/26/poverty-facts-and-stats#src1.

[56] Iyer, *Parapolitics,* p.230.

[57] This quote was told to me by Jeff Bleich, a brilliant lawyer and friend, now the United States Ambassador to Australia.

[58] Greg Mortenson, *Three Cups of Tea* (New York: Penguin, 2006), p.292.

[59] Barack Obama, *The Audacity of Hope* (New York: Crown, 2006), p.320.

[60] Al Gore, *An Inconvenient Truth* (Emmaus, PA: Rodale, 2006), p.162.

[61] Donald A. Levin, *American Scientist Magazine* (January/February 2002).

[62] *National Geographic News,* "Seafood May Be Gone by 2048, Study Says," November 2, 2006: http://news.nationalgeographic.com/news/2006/11/061102-seafood-threat.html.

[63] Levin, *American Scientist Magazine* (January/February 2002).

[64] *National Geographic News,* "Mount Kilimanjaro's Glacier Is Crumbling," September 21, 2009: http://news.nationalgeographic.com/news/2003/09/0923_030923_kilimanjaroglaciers.html.

[65] United Nations Environment Programme (UNEP): http://www.unep.org/billiontreecampaign/FactsFigures/QandA/index.asp.

[66] Mikhail Gorbachev, *The Search for a New Beginning: Developing a New Civilization* (San Francisco: Harper, 1995), p.27. ("We will meet the challenge if we become aware of the world's unity, of humankind's common destiny, and of the responsibility of every one of us for the preservation of life on Earth.")

[67] See *"Stern Review on Economics of Climate Change* (Cambridge: Cambridge University Press, 2008)," by Sir Nicholas Stern, head of the Government Economic Service and Adviser to the Government on the economics of climate change and development: http://www.hm-treasury.gov.uk/sternreview_index.htm. (Costs of mitigation of around 1% of GDP are small relative to the costs and risks of climate change that will be avoided.)

[68] Of course, judicial review is imperfect, but it generally works, even in Asian countries. See Tom Ginsburg, *Judicial Review in New Democracies, Constitutional Courts in Asian Cases* (Cambridge: Cambridge University Press, 2003), p.15.

[69] Robert A Kagan, *Adversarial Legalism, The American Way of Law* (Cambridge, MA: Harvard University Press, 1991), p.32. ("Adversarial legalism sometimes works well, yielding social benefits that far outweigh its costs; that it sometimes works badly, generating social costs that outweigh its intended benefits; and that sometimes it produces a difficult-to-evaluate mix of social costs and benefits.")

[70] Robert Scheer, *The Pornography of Power: Why Defense Spending Must Be Cut* (New York: Twelve, 2009), p.174.

[71] Pico Iyer, *The Global Soul, Jet Lag, Shopping Malls, and the Search for Home* (New York: Vintage, 2000), p.31.

[72] Sunstein, *The Second Bill of Rights,* (New York: Basic, 2004), p.2.

[73] The High Court of Justice—Queen's Bench Division, June 19, 1997, No.1990-M-NO.5724: http://www.hmcourts-service.gov.uk (October 5, 2009).

[74] *Case of Steel and Morris v. The United Kingdom,* European Court of Human Rights Portal. Fourth Section, February 15, 2005, received October 5, 2009.

[75] Helen Keller and Alec Stone Sweet, *A Europe of Rights: The Impact of the European Court of Human Rights on National Legal Systems* (Oxford: Oxford University Press, 2008). (This impressive work includes articles written by various scholars discussing legal systems throughout Europe.)

[76] For a thoughtful analysis of this "margin of appreciation," see Burleigh Wilkins, ed., *The European Convention on Human Rights* (Dubuque: Kendall/Hunt, 2008), p.23.

[77] Ralph Waldo Emerson, *Self-Reliance* (New York: Penguin, 2009), p.64 (published with President Obama's 2009 Inaugural Address).

[78] Global Issues Website: "Over 25,000 children die every day around the world. The silent killers are poverty, hunger, easily preventable

diseases and illnesses, and other related causes": http://www.globalissues.org/article/715/today-over-25000-children-died-around-the-world.

[79] Jakob Th. Moller and Alfred de Zayas, *United Nations Human Rights Committee Case Law 1977–2008* (Kehl am Rhein, Germany: Engel, 2009). (Alfred de Zayas is also a member of the Board for the 2048 Project.)

[80] For good insight as to why humans are not inherently warlike from a military man with both the training and experience to assess human character, see Paul K. Chappell, *Will War Ever End?* (Weston: Ashoka, 2009).

[81] Eleanor Roosevelt, *What I Hope to Leave Behind,* (New York: Carlson, 1995) p.188.

[82] Abbas Milani, *Lost Wisdom, Rethinking Modernity in Iran* (Washington, DC: Mage, 2004), p.21. (Democracy, rationalism and the rule of law are not strange and alien ideas to Iran, but have deep native roots in the intellectual soil of this old, enduring, and now beleaguered land.)

[83] Barack Obama, *The Inaugural Address* (quoting from Ralph Waldo Emerson, *Self-Reliance)* (New York: Penguin, 2009).

[84] Steve Martin, *Picasso at the Lapin Agile and Other Plays* (New York: Grove Press, 1996), pp.57–58.

[85] Paul Hawken, *Blessed Unrest,* (New York: Penguin, 2007), p.192.

[86] 2048 is a liberation movement, not a resistance movement. See Richard Flacks, *Making History, The American Left and the American Mind.* (New York: Columbia University Press, 1988), p.77. (People may seek new rights and entitlements or to rewrite the rules.)

[87] Eleanor Roosevelt, "My Day" (syndicated column, April 16, 1945).

[88] *Time,* December 25, 2006/January 1, 2007, p.41.

[89] Captain Paul Chappell, *Will War Ever End?* (Weston: Ashoka, 2009), p.37.

[90] Hazel Felleman, *The Best Loved Poems of the American People* (New York: Double day, 1936), pp.273–274.

[91] Allida M. Black, *Eleanor Roosevelt, Courage in Dangerous Times* (New York: Columbia University Press, 1999), p. i.

[92] There are also supplements to the curriculum such as a play written and performed by students and put on DVD for teachers to use.

[93] James McGregor Burns and Stewart Burns, *A People's Charter: The Pursuit of Rights in America* (New York: Knopf, 1991), p.20.

[94] Richard Falk, *Human Rights Horizons: The Pursuit of Justice in a Globalizing World* (New York: Routledge, 2000), p.90.

[95] David Vogel, *The Market for Virtue: The Potential and Limits of Corporate Social Responsibility* (Washington, DC: Brookings Institution Press, 2005), p.159. ("Companies can be financially disadvantaged by voluntary restrictions on where they do business.")

[96] A shining example is the late Anita Roddick. See *Brave Hearts, Rebel Spirits* (West Sussex: Anita Roddick Books, 2003), p.7.

[97] Robert F. Kennedy. University of Kansas, March 18, 1968: http://www.jfklibrary.org/Historical+Resources/Archives/Reference+Desk/Speeches/RFK/RFKSpeech68Mar18UKansas.htm. The quotation was said by the serpent in George Bernard Shaw's play *Back to Methuselah* and was used by President Kennedy in his speech to the Irish Parliament on June 28, 1963: "Speaking as an Irishman [Shaw] summed up an approach to life: 'Other people,' he said, 'see things and say: why—but I dream things that never were and say: why not.'"

[98] "Reality leaves a lot to the imagination." John Lennon: www.quotegarden.com.

[99] John Rawls, *A Theory of Justice* (Cambridge, MA: Harvard University Press, 1971).
[100] John Rawls, *Political Liberalism* (New York: Columbia University Press, 1993).
[101] John Rawls, *The Law of Peoples* (Cambridge, MA: Harvard University Press, 1999).
[102] *Id.,* at pp.136–37.
[103] William F. Felice, *The Global New Deal: Economic and Social Human Rights in World Politics* (New York: Romann & Littlefield, 2006), p.152.
[104] Rawls, *A Theory of Justice,* p.149.
[105] George Soros, *The Bubble of American Supremacy, Correcting the Misuse of American Power* (New York: Public Affairs, 2004), p.195.
[106] The National Human Rights Consultation for Australia: http://www.humanrightsconsultation.gov.au.
[107] Having reviewers for articles submitted has some definite benefits. See Cass Sunstein, *Infotopia, How Many Minds Produce Knowledge* (Oxford: Oxford University Press, 2006), pp.162–163. (Noting the success of ohmynews.com where stories are submitted by the public and then reviewed by staff, 2048 takes a similar approach.)
[108] George Soros, *George Soros on Globalization* (New York: Public Affairs, 2002), p. vii.
[109] *Id.,* at p. viii.

[110] John Humphrey was the director of research for the working group for the Universal Declaration. He had a staff of thirty and did a superb job of collecting information about the various bills of rights adopted in numerous countries to see what they did, or did not, have in common. This is the seminal research work that 2048 and the International Convention carry on today.

[111] The International Law Commission considers proposals for the progressive development of international law referred by the General Assembly (article 16) or submitted by members of the United Nations, the principal organs of the United Nations other than the General Assembly, specialized agencies or official bodies established by intergovernmental agreements to encourage the progressive development and codification of international law (article 17).

[112] Charter of the United Nations, article 13(1)(a).

[113] Agenda for Human Rights: www.udhr60.ch.

[114] Project on International Courts and Tribunals (PICT): www.pict-pcti.org.

[115] Referring to the U.S. Constitution in his 1801 annual address to Congress, Thomas Jefferson said, "It is the ligament which binds us into one nation." First Annual Message to Congress, December 8, 1801, Kaminski, *The*

Quotable Jefferson, p.51. So too the International Convention will be the ligament that binds us into an international community based on the rule of law.

[116] For a good discussion of how case law can develop through international courts and tribunals, see, *The International Judge: An Introduction to the Men and Women Who Decide the World's Cases,* Daniel Terris, Cesare P.R. Romano, Leigh Swigart, and Sonia Sotomayor (Waltham, Brandeis, 2007).

[117] Black, *Courage in a Dangerous World,* p.190. (Eleanor wrote in her "My Day" column on April 9, 1953, that she was "embarrassed" that the United States would not support legally enforceable human rights. 2048 helps to keep alive the beauty of her dream.)

[118] It takes time to develop expertise. See Malcolm Gladwell, *Outliers,* (New York: Little, Brown, 2008), p.40. ("In fact, researchers have settled on what they believe is the magic number for expertise: ten thousand hours.")

PHOTO CREDITS

Introduction: Martin Luther King Jr.—© Steve Schapiro/Corbis

Chapter 1: Elie Wiesel—United Nations Images

Chapter 2: Robert Haas—© Louie Psihoyos/Corbis

Chapter 3: Franklin Roosevelt—© AP Photo

Chapter 4: Nelson Mandela—© Greg Marinovich/Sygma/Corbis

Chapter 5: Gandhi—© Margaret Bourke-White/Time Life Pictures/Getty Images

Chapter 6: Mother Theresa—© Eddie Adams/AP Images

Chapter 7: Al Gore—© Valery Hache/AFP/Getty Images

Chapter 8: Mikhail Gorbachev—© Bernard Bisson and Thierry Orban/Sygma/Corbis

Chapter 9: René Cassin—United Nations Images

Chapter 10: Eleanor Roosevelt—United Nations Images

Chapter 11: Charles Malik—© Bettmann/Corbis

Chapter 12: Oscar Arias—United Nations Images

Chapter 13: P.C. Chang—United Nations Images

Chapter 14: Tim Berners-Lee—© Elise Amendola/AP Images

Chapter 15: Dag Hammarskjold—United Nations Images

Conclusion: John Humphrey—© Nick Deichmann, McGill News/McGill University Archives

ACKNOWLEDGMENTS

This book is about an ongoing international social movement. As with any movement, there are numerous people and organizations involved and I can't hope to thank all of them. I am only acknowledging a fraction of people who have made *2048,* both the book and the Project, possible. I appreciate all who have been and remain involved.

There are several people who have been essential throughout. My stepfather, David Roberts, has been a central pillar. He has been a good editor among his many supportive roles, but most of all he has encouraged me to persevere when times were difficult. John Esterle of the Whitman Institute has been the other key pillar by providing catalytic funding and complementing it with sage advice over several years. Professor David Caron at Boalt Hall has been a teacher, advisor and friend over many years and degrees. But for his willingness to fill in after Frank Newman's death (I'm also deeply indebted to Frank), I would not have been able to take this path less traveled which has briar, but is rewarding. Jonathan Simon, the Principal Investigator for the 2048 Project is an excellent leader. I've benefited immeasurably from the keenness of his intellect, steadfastness and friendship. Neither this book nor the Project would have been able to go forward without him. I also want to thank Christopher Edley, the Dean of Berkeley Law. In addition to building new structures for the school, he has built space for long-range cutting-edge research projects such as 2048. Both through physical space and intellectually, his imprint will be lengthy.

Mishana Hosseinioun has been integral to the development of *2048* at every level from basic organizing to the sharp thinking that has carried her to work on her doctorate at Oxford. Bruna Molina, our 2048 Geneva representative, is our modern day Eleanor Roosevelt. Her charm and extensive connections within the United Nations has kept 2048 moving forward at crucial junctures. Alfred de Zayas, an attorney who worked for years with the Human Rights Committee, works with Bruna in Geneva and it is excellent to have his keen insights and quick wit for our weekly conference calls.

I am fortunate to have close friends who have also been 2048 Board members and reliable supporters over the years. Frank Kelly has been an inspiration as an author and an intellect. Professors Marc McGinnes and Burleigh Wilkins sparked my genuine interest in law and philosophy many years ago when I was a student at UCSB, and remain advisors and friends today. Nobel laureate, Walter Kohn, along with tea, has shared a vision as broad as the view from his Santa Barbara office. I've had tofu and eggs many times with Carrie Avery, President of the Durfee Foundation, and mussels for birthdays with Jeff Bleich, the United States Ambassador to Australia. Their ideas are present in the book and the endnotes acknowledging them are a small reflection of their contributions.

E.J. Flynn has shared his United Nations insights and his time in Geneva. He is always good company as well as a very good lawyer. Robert Rosenthal, Executive Director for the Center for Investigative Reporting, through edits and commentary has infused my writing with passion and purpose, two of his fine qualities. Andrew Thompson, a successful businessman and politician, has brought a mix of the local with the international that *2048* strives to achieve.

The staff of 2048 is essential to the success of the Project and book. The work of Matt Schwoebel, our Program Director, is reflected in both the wording of this book and the implementation of the ideas within it. We have had a host of interns, and I am especially grateful to Maya Rupert who went on to a successful law career, Cary Levine who went on in business and Ryan Cohen who did an excellent, and timely, job editing *2048.* Christina Kaspar, Jessica Chen, Alexandra Aja, Margaux Fitoussi, Daphna Davidovits, Heather Thibeault, Shafinaaz Kamrul, Romina Filippou, Benjamin Omidvari, Farid Golshani and Ashley Warner have also made valuable contributions both to the book and to the Project.

I also appreciate my wife, Jennifer, sons Stephen and William, and daughter, Maria. I hope this book will improve their lives, and the lives of families internationally.

Finally, I'm fortunate to be working with great people professionally for the preparation and production of this book. Steve Piersanti and Jeevan

Sivasubramaniam at Berrett Koehler live by their mission to "create a world that works for all," and *2048* can do that. Book designers, Diane Platner and Richard Wilson created a captivating jacketless cover and the marketing team of Kristen Franz, Jeremy Sullivan, Peter Cavagnaro and Katie Sheehan has effectively launched *2048* into the marketplace of ideas.

Michael Larsen, my agent, believes that "the right book can change the world." He gave *2048* its start through his own writing, conferences, friendship and hard work. Vicki Weiland has been an inspirational and meticulous editor for text and images. Her dedication to continue editing from a hospital bed when she was stricken with an unusual illness is representative of the finest human qualities that we are trying to draw out with this book. Minette Siegel has shown her skill and experience by finding images that complement the text and make the book memorable. Right to the finish Aline Magee and Valerie Brewster have been effecive at sewarding the book to its final completion. My thanks to all of you.

2048 Follow-up

If 2048 inspires you, here are suggestions for how to help:

1. Visit the www.2048.berkeley.edu website for more info, book reviews, events, and ideas. The website is the heart of the 2048 Project, and you can always find something to do there.
2. Become a member of the 2048 Project. Membership is free, but everyone who contributes $20.48 receives a free copy of the beautiful hardcover edition of *2048,* a $22.95 value. Every book for members has been signed with a special inscription from the author. It's easy to join—just go to the website and click on the big green button at the top of the screen, and welcome to the 2048 Project!
3. Attend author's events for *2048.* There is an events calendar on the website so you can see where Kirk Boyd will be speaking. In addition, if you have ideas about groups of at least 20 people whom Kirk can speak with, then please e-mail

information about the group and help coordinate an event.

4. Go to your local independent or chain bookstore and buy a copy of the book. If the book is not there, ask the staff to put two on the shelf and promise you'll buy one of them. *2048* is a movement, and this is what it takes. Going to the store is also good support for bookstores. The only reason we have bookstores is because people go and buy books from them! There is nothing wrong with buying online, but let's keep our bookstores alive, too.
5. Suggest *2048* to a friend, colleague, book club, church, civic group, synagogue, mosque, university or high school class, or any group interested in education, literacy, politics, law or cross-cultural issues. If you purchase a book from us on our website to give to someone, or if you give someone the book you bought for yourself, tell us and we will give you one for free. *2048* is the story of a social movement, and nothing will further the movement faster or farther than giving someone a book.
6. Check to see if *2048* is in your local libraries, including both your public libraries and your school libraries. If it is not, ask the librarian to order it for the public library or school library. If they lack funds but will promise to put the book into circulation, send us an e-mail, and we will send them a book for free.

7. Write *2048* reviews for Amazon.com, Barnes & Noble, Borders, or any other bookseller or blog. Your reviews will help create a buzz about the book and encourage others to read it. As with the input to the International Convention, feel free to make critical as well as positive comments.
8. Make a financial contribution. It takes funding to disseminate information about 2048 and to organize the students and people from all professions who are participating in the 2048 movement. In particular, there are a lot of translation and website costs to keep our dialogue going and growing, and to include students in all countries. All donations are fully tax-deductible, and you can specify what aspect of the 2048 Project work you would like your money to go toward.
9. For media inquiries, please contact the Publicity Department of Berrett-Koehler: ksheehan@bkpub.com or (415)743-6477.
10. For more information, contact:

2048 Project
Berkeley Law School
2850 Telegraph Ave., Suite 500
Berkeley, CA 94705
(510)642-5924
www.2048.berkeley.edu

ABOUT THE AUTHOR

Kirk Boyd is the executive director of the 2048 Project at the University of California, Berkeley, School of Law. Kirk's specialty is the legal enforcement of international human rights, which reflects his training as a trial and appellate lawyer and his academic work. He has his BA in political science from the University of California, Santa Barbara, and his JD, LLM, and JSD from the University of California, Berkeley. He has taught at U.C. Santa Barbara and U.C. Berkeley over many years, including courses on international human rights, international law, civil rights, constitutional law, and free speech. He is currently teaching in the Legal Studies Program at U.C. Berkeley.

Kirk began his career with the law firm Morrison & Foerster before forming a partnership with others, Boyd, Huffman, and Williams. He continues to handle a few legal cases on the forefront of civil rights and human rights and he has argued in courts at every level, including the U.S. Supreme Court.

Kirk works with numerous human rights organizations and bar association groups and is a member of several service groups including U.N. Associations and Rotary International. He is a frequent speaker at conferences, on panels, and in classrooms, and he welcomes invitations to speak about the 2048 Project.

ABOUT BERRETT-KOEHLER PUBLISHERS

Berrett-Koehler is an independent publisher dedicated to an ambitious mission: Creating a World That Works for All.

We believe that to truly create a better world, action is needed at all levels—individual, organizational, and societal. At the individual level, our publications help people align their lives with their values and with their aspirations for a better world. At the organizational level, our publications promote progressive leadership and management practices, socially responsible approaches to business, and humane and effective organizations. At the societal level, our publications advance social and economic justice, shared prosperity, sustainability, and new solutions to national and global issues.

A major theme of our publications is "Opening Up New Space." They challenge conventional thinking, introduce new ideas, and foster positive change. Their common quest is changing the underlying beliefs, mindsets, and structures that keep generating the same cycles of problems, no matter who our leaders are or what improvement programs we adopt.

We strive to practice what we preach—to operate our publishing company in line with the ideas in our books. At the core of our approach is *stewardship,* which we define as a deep sense of responsibility to administer the company for the benefit of all of our "stakeholder" groups: authors, customers, employees, investors, service providers, and the communities and environment around us.

We are grateful to the thousands of readers, authors, and other friends of the company who consider themselves to be part of the "BK Community." We hope that you, too, will join us in our mission.

A BK CURRENTS BOOK

This book is part of our BK Currents series. BK Currents books advance social and economic justice by exploring the critical intersections between business and society. Offering a unique combination of thoughtful analysis and progressive alternatives, BK Currents books promote positive change at the national and global levels. To find out more, visit www.bkcurrents.com.

BE CONNECTED

VISIT OUR WEBSITE

Go to www.bkconnection.com to read exclusive previews and excerpts of new books, find detailed information on all Berrett-Koehler titles and authors, browse subject-area libraries of books, and get special discounts.

SUBSCRIBE TO OUR FREE E-NEWSLETTER

Be the first to hear about new publications, special discount offers, exclusive articles, news about bestsellers, and more! Get on the list for our free e-newsletter by going to www.bkconnection.com.

GET QUANTITY DISCOUNTS

Berrett-Koehler books are available at quantity discounts for orders of ten or more copies. Please call us toll-free at (800)929-2929 or email us at bkp.orders@aidcvt.com.

HOST A READING GROUP

For tips on how to form and carry on a book reading group in your workplace or community, see our website at www.bkconnection.com.

JOIN THE BK COMMUNITY

Thousands of readers of our books have become part of the "BK Community" by participating in events featuring our authors, reviewing draft manuscripts of forthcoming books, spreading the word about their favorite books, and supporting our publishing program in other ways. If you would like to join the BK Community, please contact us at bkcommunity@bkpub.com.

C

D

E

G

R

U

Books For ALL Kinds of Readers

Printed in Dunstable, United Kingdom

91220092R00174